50 Quick & Easy Computer Activities for Kids

by Tammy Worcester

VISIONS

Technology in Education

Project Coordinator/Production
Ken Harvey

Copy Editor
Sharleen Nelson

Cover Design
Tim Yost

Copyright Notice

Publisher: Visions Technology in Education

P.O. Box 70479
Eugene, OR 97401
Phone: 541.349.0905
Fax: 541.349.0944
Email: info@visteched.net

Order desk: 800.877.0858
Order fax: 800.816.0695
Web site: www.toolsforteachers.com

ISBN: 1-58912-234-8
SKU #: 91240

From the Publisher

Visions Technology in Education develops and publishes technology rich educational material for teachers, students, parents' and educational leaders. By producing field-tested resources to assist in the teaching/learning process, Visions aims to utilize technology to better serve students and educators alike.

Our wide variety of books and software promotes interactive learning on a personal basis as well as in a classroom or training context. With the increasing expectations placed upon educators to meet the needs of special learning groups as well as striving to stay current with rapidly changing technology, we seek to select quality materials that assist you in both endeavors.

Visions' goal is to provide affordable resources that "help you help others"—today and tomorrow. Please let us know how we can be more effective by sharing your ideas and opinions with us.

Table of Contents

Word Processing

1   Riddle Mixup...1
2   Story Swap...3
3   Synonym Switch...5
4   TALL Tales...7
5   Zoo Diorama..9

Desktop Publishing

6   ABC Quilt...11
7   Book Review Bookmark...13
8   Candy "Rappers"..15
9   Famous Person Fact Flipper...17
10 Picture Post Card..19
11 State Mini-Books...21
12 I'm T-rrific...23
13 Weather Acrostics..25
14 Zip-Up Leaf Displays...27

Painting / Drawing

15 Chinese Lantern..29
16 Create Your Own Animal!..31
17 Draw Me!...33
18 Following Directions...35
19 Shape Poem...37

Spreadsheet

20 Daily Temperature Chart..39
21 Eye Color Bar Chart..41
22 Magic Square...43
23 Pizza Pie Graph..45
24 Planet Weigh In..47
25 The Power of a Penny...49
26 Wish List Calculator...51

Inspiration / Kidspiration

27 Brainstorming!...53
28 Color Quatrain...55
29 Debating an Issue..57
30 Map-It...59
31 Now and Then...61
32 Number Autobiography...63
33 Story Map Mobile...65
34 Wouldn't It Be Cool If...67

Slide Show

35 Choose Your Own Ending..69
36 I'm Thankful For..71
37 Idiom Slide Show..73
38 Sing-Along Slide Show...75
39 Point of View Poem...77
40 What Animal Am I?...79

Internet

41 Classmates Crossword...81
42 Weather Cryptogram..83
43 Teacher's Helper Hotlists...85
44 Online Mad Libs...87
45 Interactive Internet Activities...89
46 Personalized Stories...91

Crafts / Gifts

47 Coupon Booklets..93
48 Key Ring for Dad..95
49 Magnet for Mother..97
50 Sun Catchers...99

Riddle Mix-up

Grade Level:
- K
- 1
- 2
- • 3
- • 4
- • 5
- • 6

Content Area:
- Math
- • Language Arts
- Social Studies
- Science
- • Cross Curricular

Multiple Intelligences:
- • Verbal / Linguistic
- • Logical / Mathematical
- Spatial
- Bodily / Kinesthetic
- Musical
- Interpersonal
- Intrapersonal
- Naturalist

CD-ROM Templates:
- • 01Riddle.doc - Microsoft Word
- • 01Riddleb.doc - Microsoft Word
- • 01Riddle.cwk - AppleWorks
- • 01Riddleb.cwk - AppleWorks

Overview:
In this activity, students will use the cut and paste functions to put "mixed up" riddles in order. Then they will learn how to copy and paste an image from the Internet.

Software:
Microsoft Word or AppleWorks Word Processing

ISTE Standards:
- • Students are proficient in the use of technology.
- • Students develop positive attitudes toward technology.

The Teacher's Role:
1. The teacher provides each student with an electronic copy of the mixed up riddle file. *Note - the file can be loaded onto each computer through a network server or using a floppy disk, CD, or removable drive. Your tech support person may be able to help!*
2. The teacher demonstrates how to cut and paste text.
   (The teacher may want to explain that each computer has something called a clipboard. Whenever a user pulls down the Edit menu to Copy (or Cut), the selected item is placed on the clipboard -- and it is just waiting to be pasted somewhere! The item remains on the clipboard until something else is cut or copied -- or until the computer is shut down. It is important to know that the clipboard can only hold ONE thing!)
3. The teacher demonstrates how to copy an image from the Internet. *Note - if Internet access is not available, students may use clip art from their word processing program.*

Student Instructions:

Putting the riddles in order:

1. Open the Riddle Mixup file.
2. Click and drag to select the desired block of text.
3. Pull down the **Edit** menu to **Cut**.
4. Insert the cursor where you want the text to appear.
5. Pull down the **Edit** menu to **Paste**.
6. Repeat steps 2-5 until all questions and answers are in order.
7. Make your document look cool by changing the fonts, sizes, and colors! Add a title too.
8. SAVE!

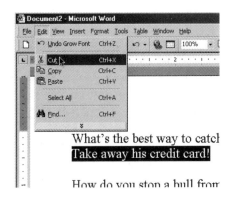

Adding an image:

1. Open your browser (Internet Explorer or Netscape) and go to a clip art site such as:
   http://www.school.discovery.com/clipart
   http://www.awesomeclipartforkids.com/
2. Browse to find an appropriate image.
3. Position your cursor directly over the image.
4. On a Macintosh computer, click and hold the mouse button (or Control-click).
   On a Windows computer, click the right mouse button.
   A menu should appear.
5. Choose **"Copy Image"** or **"Copy"**.
   (This places the image in your computer's clipboard!)
6. Return to your riddle document.
7. Insert your cursor where you want the image to appear.
8. Pull down the **Edit** menu to **Paste**.
9. SAVE!

Student Challenge Question:

What's the difference between the "**Copy**" and the "**Cut**" functions?

Options / Extensions:

- Instead of using the provided riddle file, students could each type 4 or 5 of their favorite riddles and "mix them up". Then have the students trade computers to complete the task. (You may want to have some riddle books available.)
- Students may want to use keyboard shortcuts instead of pulling down menus. (ex. Control + X to cut.)
- Students may want to try dragging and dropping instead of using the cut and paste options.
- This activity could be done using vocabulary words and definitions or using questions and answers that are content-related. Or, mix up a story and have students put it back in order! Or, mix up some step-by-step instructions...

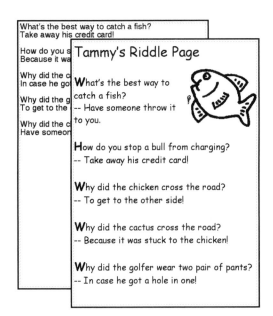

Story Swap

Grade Level:
- K (See extensions)
- 1 (See extensions)
- 2 (See extensions)
- 3
- 4
- 5
- 6

Content Area:
Math
- Language Arts
Social Studies
Science
- Cross Curricular

Multiple Intelligences:
- Verbal / Linguistic
  Logical / Mathematical
  Spatial
  Bodily / Kinesthetic
  Musical
- Interpersonal
  Intrapersonal
  Naturalist

Overview:
Each student begins a story on his/her computer. After a few minutes, students rotate to the computer on their right and continue adding to each other's stories.

ISTE Standards:
- Students are proficient in the use of technology.
- Students develop positive attitudes toward technology uses that support lifelong learning, collaboration, personal pursuits, and productivity.
- Students use productivity tools to collaborate in constructing technology-enhanced models, prepare publications, and produce other creative works.

Software:
AppleWorks Word Processing or Microsoft Word

The Teacher's Role:
1. The teacher will explain the activity and will set any ground rules.
2. The teacher will set the timer and will tell the students when to switch computers.
3. The teacher will demonstrate (if necessary) how to change fonts, sizes, styles, etc.
4. The teacher will show the students how to add clip art. (optional)

Student Instructions:

Creating the collaborative story:
1. Open a word processing document.
2. Begin typing a story (just make it up!).
3. When the teacher tells you, get up and move to the computer at your right.
4. Read what has been written.
5. Continue to add to the story.
6. Repeat steps 3-5 until the teacher tells you to stop.

Fancying the document:
1. Return to the computer where you started.
2. Read the story.
3. Add an appropriate title at the top of the story.
4. Change the fonts, sizes, colors, etc. if you want.
5. Add clip art:
   AppleWorks:
   a. Pull down the **File** menu to **Library** or **Show Clippings**.
   b. Choose an image and click **Insert** (or drag it onto your screen).
   Microsoft Word:
   a. Pull down the **Insert** menu to **Picture** and pull over to **Clip Art**.
   b. Choose an image and follow the on-screen prompts to insert it.
6. SAVE!
7. Print and share!!!

Extensions:
• Students can create a collaborative report. The first student starts by typing one fact about a subject (could be a person, place, animal, thing, etc.). Students rotate around, adding their own facts to the report.

• **For younger students:**
   • Instead of typing a story, younger students could open a painting / drawing program and begin to draw a picture. Then they can switch computers and continue to add to the masterpiece!
   • OR have young students type ONE word and then rotate. The challenge is to try to create complete sentences.

Pleaase do not copy.

Synonym Switch

Grade Level:
K
1
• 2
• 3
• 4
• 5
• 6

Content Area:
Math
• Language Arts
Social Studies
Science
• Cross Curricular

Multiple Intelligences:
• Verbal / Linguistic
Logical / Mathematical
Spatial
Bodily / Kinesthetic
Musical
Interpersonal
Intrapersonal
Naturalist

CD-ROM Templates:
• 03synonyms.doc - Microsoft Word
• 03cynonyms.cwk - AppleWorks

Overview:
In this activity, students will use the thesaurus of their word processing program to apply alternative word choice to sentences.

Software:
Microsoft PowerPoint or AppleWorks Word Processing

ISTE Standards:
• Students develop positive attitudes toward technology uses that support lifelong learning, collaboration, personal pursuits, and productivity.
• Students use technology tools to enhance learning, increase productivity, and promote creativity.

The Teacher's Role:
1. The teacher will provide the students with one or more sentences that have common, overused words.
2. The teacher will instruct the students to type the sentence.
3. The teacher will show the students how to copy and paste the sentence.
4. The teacher will show the students how to use the thesaurus to change at least 3 words in each sentence.

Student Instructions:

Getting Ready:
1. Type the sentence that your teacher gives you.
2. Click and drag to highlight the entire sentence.
3. Pull down the **Edit** menu to **Copy**.
4. Click at the end of the sentence and press the Return or Enter key on your keyboard.
5. Pull down the **Edit** menu to **Paste**.

Switching the synonyms:
1. Highlight a common word in the second sentence.
2. Use the thesaurus to change the word to one that sounds better.
   (See instructions below.)
3. Repeat for at least two other words in the sentence.
4. SAVE!

Microsoft Word Thesaurus:
1. Highlight a word.
2. Pull down the **Tools** menu to **Language** and pull over to **Thesaurus**.
   OR
   Press the Shift and F7 keys on your keyboard.
3. Choose a synonym that sounds good.
4. Click the **Replace** button.

AppleWorks Thesaurus:
1. Highlight a word.
2. Pull down the **Edit** menu to **Writing Tools** and pull over to **Thesaurus**.
   OR
   Press the Apple, Shift, and Z keys on your keyboard.
3. Choose a synonym that sounds good.
4. Click the **Replace** button.

Extensions:
• Students could work in pairs or teams to complete the activity.
• Students could use the thesaurus to choose better words in their own stories.

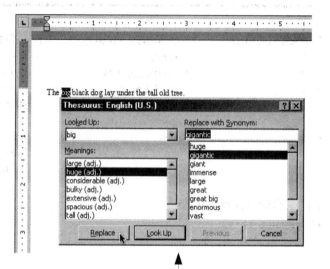

Microsoft Word Thesaurus
AppleWorks Thesaurus

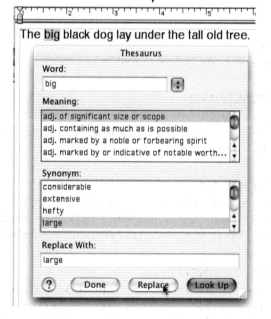

Before:
The big black dog lay under the tall old tree.

After:
The large black hound reclined under the towering old tree.

TALL Tales!

4

Grade Level:
- K
- 1
- • 2
- • 3
- • 4
- • 5
- • 6

Content Area:
- Math
- • Language Arts
- • Social Studies
- Science
- • Cross Curricular

Multiple Intelligences:
- • Verbal / Linguistic
- Logical / Mathematical
- • Spatial
- Bodily / Kinesthetic
- Musical
- • Interpersonal
- Intrapersonal
- • Naturalist

CD-ROM Templates:
- • 04talltale.doc - Microsoft Word
- • 04talltale.cwk - AppleWorks

Overview:
Students will write a tall tale and enter it into a word processing document. Then they will divide the story into columns; print; cut the columns apart; and tape the "strips" end-to-end to create a really TALL, tall tale!

Software:
Microsoft Word or AppleWorks Word Processing

ISTE Standards:
- • Students are proficient in the use of technology.
- • Students use technology tools to enhance learning, increase productivity, and promote creativity.

Web Resources:
Tall Tales - http://www.hasd.org/ges/talltale/talltale.htm
American Folklore - http://www.americanfolklore.net/tt.html
Paul Bunyan Trail - http://www.paulbunyantrail.com/talltale.html

The Teacher's Role:
1. The teacher will provide tall tales for the students to read.
2. The teacher will discuss the characteristics of tall tales.
3. The teacher will direct the students in writing tall tales of their own (individually or in teams).
4. The teacher will direct the students to type their tall tales into a word processing document. (Note -- if students have difficulty with keyboarding, the teacher may want to have an adult or older student type it.)
5. The teacher will demonstrate how to divide the document into columns.

Student Instructions:

AppleWorks:

1. Write a tall tale of your own and enter it into an AppleWorks word processing document.
2. Pull down the **Format** menu to **Document**.
3. Change all of the margins to .5 inches.
4. Click the **column icon** in the tool bar to divide the page into three columns.
5. Make the font size larger so that your tale is about 2 pages.
6. SAVE.
7. Print.
8. Cut the columns apart and trim so that the "strips" are the same width.
9. Tape the strips in order end to end to create a really TALL, tall tale!
10. SAVE!

Microsoft Word:

1. Write a tall tale of your own and enter it into a Word document.
2. Pull down the **File** menu to **Page Setup**. Click the Margins tab.
3. Change all of the top, bottom, left, and right margins to .5 inches.
4. Pull down the **Format** menu to **Columns**.
5. Click to choose 3 columns.
6. Change the size of the text so that your tale is about 2 pages.
7. SAVE.
8. Print.
9. Cut the columns apart and trim so that the "strips" are the same width.
10. Tape the strips in order end to end to create a really TALL, tall tale!
11. SAVE!

Extensions:

• Hang the Tall tales in the hallway or library for a great display!
• Students could add hats and feet to their tall tales.
• Roll the tall tale strip and tie with a string or ribbon to send home.

AppleWorks Column Icon

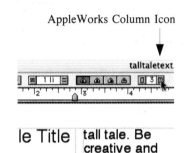

Microsoft Word Columns

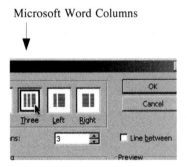

Tall Tale!

In this area you would enter your own tall tale. Be creative and imaginative. Exaggerate all you want! In this area you would enter your own tall tale. Be creative and imaginative. Exaggerate all you want! In this area you would enter your own tall tale. Be creative and imaginative. Exaggerate all you want! In this area you would enter your own tall tale. Be creative and imaginative.

Exaggerate all you want! In this area you would enter your own tall tale. Be creative and imaginative. Exaggerate all you want! In this area you would enter your own tall tale. Be creative and imaginative. Exaggerate all you want! In this area you would enter your own tall tale. Be creative and imaginative. Exaggerate all you want! In this area you would enter your own tall tale. Be creative and imaginative. Exaggerate all you want!

In this area you would enter your own tall tale. Be creative and imaginative. Exaggerate all you want! In this area you would enter your own tall tale. Be creative and imaginative. Exaggerate all you want! In this area you would enter your own tall tale. Be creative and imaginative. Exaggerate all you want! In this area you would enter your own tall tale. Be creative and imaginative.

Exaggerate all you want! In this area you would enter your own tall tale. Be creative and imaginative. Exaggerate all you want! In this area you would enter your own tall tale. Be creative and imaginative. Exaggerate all you want! In this area you would enter your own tall tale. Be creative and imaginative. Exaggerate all you want! In this area you would enter your own tall tale. Be creative and imaginative. Exaggerate all you want! In this area you would enter your own tall tale. Be creative and imaginative. Exaggerate all you want!

Exaggerate all you want! In this area you would enter your own tall tale. Be creative and imaginative. Exaggerate all you want! In this area you would enter your own tall tale. Be creative and imaginative. Exaggerate all you want! In this area you would enter your own tall tale. Be creative and imaginative. Exaggerate all you want! In this area you would enter your own tall tale. Be creative and imaginative. Exaggerate all you want!

Zoo Diorama

5

Grade Level:
- K (with help)
- 1 (with help)
- 2
- 3
- 4
- 5
- 6

Content Area:
Math
- Language Arts
Social Studies
- Science
- Cross Curricular

Multiple Intelligences:
- Verbal / Linguistic
Logical / Mathematical
- Spatial
- Bodily / Kinesthetic
Musical
Interpersonal
Intrapersonal
- Naturalist

CD-ROM Templates:
• zoo.doc - Microsoft Word
• zoo.cwk - AppleWorks

Overview:
Students "capture" an animal from the Internet and print the picture. They also choose a "wow" fact about the animal and type it in a word processing document. The picture is pasted to the back of the inside of a shoe box and bars are added to the front to look like a cage in a zoo. The "wow" fact is printed and cut to create a sign which is posted on the bars of the cage.

Software:
Microsoft Word or AppleWorks; Internet

ISTE Standards:
• Students use technology to locate, evaluate, and collect information from a variety of sources.
• Students use technology tools to enhance learning, increase productivity, and promote creativity.

Web Resources:
• Pics 4 Learning - http://www.pics4learning.com/
• The Amazing Picture Machine - http://www.ncrtec.org/picture.htm
• Yahooligans Animal Resources- http://www.yahooligans.com/content/animals/
• Seaworld - http://www.seaworld.org/infobook.html
• Discovery Channel Animals - http://animal.discovery.com/

The Teacher's Role:
1. The teacher will demonstrate how to search for a picture on the Internet and how to print it.
2. The teacher will provide web sites, books, videos, and other resources that contain interesting information about animals.
3. The teacher will lead the students through choosing one "wow" fact about their chosen animal. *(A "wow" fact is something that is really unusual or awesome about the animal. When people hear the fact, they will say, "Wow!")*
4. The teacher will demonstrate how to enter the "wow" fact in a text box.
5. The teacher will show the students how to assemble their dioramas.

Materials Needed:
Shoe box for each student or team
Construction paper
Hole punch (optional)
Drinking straws (optional)

Student Instructions:

Capturing the Animal:
1. Choose an animal.
2. Find a picture of the animal on the Internet.
3. Print the picture and cut it to fit the shoe box.

Creating the Sign:
1. Choose a "wow" fact about your animal.
2. Open an Appleworks Drawing program or Microsoft Word.
3. Click to select the text tool (AppleWorks) or the text box (Microsoft Word).
4. Click and drag to create a "box" on your screen.
5. Enter your animal's name in the box.
6. Below the animal's name, type "Captured by 'yourname'".
7. Type your "wow" fact.
8. Change the font, sizes, and colors if you want.
9. SAVE! Print and cut to create a sign.

Creating the cage:
1. Cut construction paper into 1/2 inch strips.
2. Glue or tape the strips to the front of the shoe box to create bars.
3. Cut a piece of construction paper a little larger than your "wow" fact.
4. Glue your fact onto the construction paper to create a sign.
5. Glue your sign to the bars.
Or
1. Use a hole punch to punch holes in the top and bottom of the shoe box (near the front).
2. Insert drinking straws for the bars.

AppleWorks
Text Tool

Microsoft Word
Text Box

Ln 1 Text Box

Giraffe
Captured by Tammy

Did you know???
A mother giraffe often gives birth
while standing so that the newborn's
first experience outside the womb is a
6 foot drop!

Options / Extensions:
- The teacher can assign animals, or students can choose their own.
- Display the dioramas on a table, or hang on a wall. *(Use thumbtacks or pins to attach to wall or bulletin board BEFORE adding the bars!)*
- Have students add a "Captured from: www.websiteaddress.com" line to their sign, so they can practice giving credit for web resources.
- Create an aquarium display with ocean animals and cover with plastic wrap or cellophane instead!

ABC Quilt

Grade Level:
- K
- 1
- 2
- 3
- 4
- 5
- 6

Content Area:
- Math
- Language Arts
- Social Studies
- Science
- Cross Curricular

Multiple Intelligences:
- Verbal / Linguistic
- Logical / Mathematical
- Spatial
- Bodily / Kinesthetic
- Musical
- Interpersonal
- Intrapersonal
- Naturalist

Overview:
In this activity, students will design "quilt blocks" for each letter of the alphabet. The blocks will be printed and then taped together to create an ABC quilt!

Software:
Kid Pix is probably best for young students, but any program that has drawing and text options will do.

ISTE Standards:
- Students are proficient in the use of technology.
- Students use technology tools to enhance learning, increase productivity, and promote creativity.

The Teacher's Role:
1. The teacher will assign one letter to each student or lead the students through choosing a letter of the alphabet. *(Students could draw a letter out of a hat!)*
2. The teacher will demonstrate how to use Kid Pix (or other program) to add the letter and a picture.
3. The teacher will help the students to print their quilt block.
4. The teacher will assist the students in putting the quilt together.

Student Instructions:

1. Think about your letter of the alphabet. What things begin with that letter?
2. Open a Kid Pix document.
3. Use the text tool to add your letter to the screen.
4. Make your letter larger.
5. Draw a picture of something that begins with your letter, or

   use the rubber stamp tool to add pictures that begin with your letter.
6. SAVE and print.
7. If you don't have a color printer, use markers or crayons to color the page.
8. After everyone in the class is done, help the teacher put your "blocks" together to create a quilt.

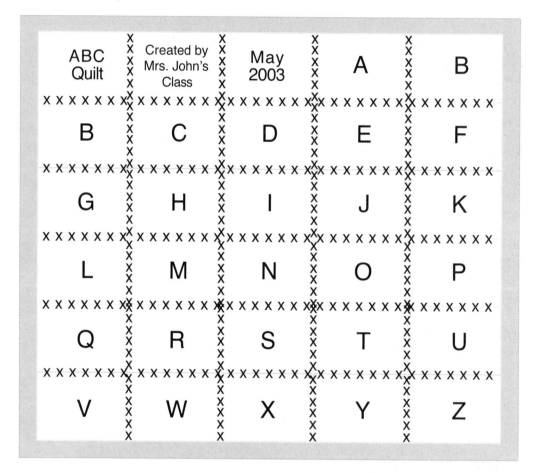

Extensions:

• Use a marker to draw "X's" on the quilt "seams".
• Add a border to the quilt using bulletin board paper or bulletin board trim.
• Purchase printable fabric sheets at a craft / hobby / quilt / fabric store. Print onto fabric sheets and sew together to make a real quilt!

Book Review Bookmark

Grade Level:
- K
- 1
- • 2
- • 3
- • 4
- • 5
- • 6

Content Area:
- Math
- • Language Arts
- Social Studies
- Science
- • Cross Curricular

Multiple Intelligences:
- • Verbal / Linguistic
- Logical / Mathematical
- • Spatial
- Bodily / Kinesthetic
- Musical
- Interpersonal
- Intrapersonal
- Naturalist

CD-ROM Templates:
- • 07bookmark.ppt - Microsoft PowerPoint
- • 07bookmark.cwk - AppleWorks

Overview:
In this activity, students will create and print 4 bookmarks with information about a favorite book.

Software:
Microsoft PowerPoint or AppleWorks Drawing

ISTE Standards:
- • Use keyboards and other common input and output devices efficiently and effectively.
- • Use technology tools for individual and collaborative writing, communication, and publishing activities.

Web Resources:
Amazon - http://www.amazon.com

The Teacher's Role:
1. The teacher will show the students how to set up their bookmark document. (See student instructions.)
2. The teacher will demonstrate how to find a picture of a book cover using the Amazon Web site or another Web site.
3. The teacher will show the students how to copy the picture of the book cover and paste it onto their bookmarks.
4. The teacher will show the students how to add text to their bookmarks.
5. The teacher will demonstrate how to copy and paste to create 4 identical bookmarks.

Student Instructions:

Setting up the bookmark document:

Appleworks:

1. Open an Appleworks Draw program.
2. Pull down the **File** menu to **Page Setup** to turn the page sideways (horizontal or landscape).
3. Pull down the **Format** menu to **Rulers** and choose to **Show Rulers**.
4. Pull down the **Format** menu to **Document** and set all margins to .5.
5. Use the line tool to draw vertical lines to divide the document into 4 equal parts. (Each part will be a bookmark.)

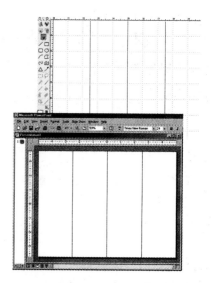

Microsoft PowerPoint:

1. Open a blank PowerPoint slide.
2. If the rulers are not showing, pull down the **View** menu to **Ruler**.
3. Use the line tool to draw vertical lines to divide the document into 4 equal parts. (Each part will be a bookmark.)

Copying a picture of the book cover:

1. Open a Web site such as www.amazon.com/
2. Enter the title of your book in the search window; click Go.
3. Find a picture of your book cover.
4. Position your cursor directly over the image.
5. On a *Macintosh* computer, click and hold the mouse button (or control-click).
   On a *Windows* computer, click the right mouse button. A menu should appear.
6. Choose "Copy Image" or "Copy".

Creating the first bookmark:

1. Return to your bookmark document.
2. Pull down the **Edit** menu to **Paste**.
3. Move the image into the first bookmark space.
4. Use a text box (or boxes) to add the book title, the author, and a brief review
5. Change the fonts, sizes, and alignments to make it look nice.

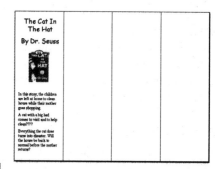

Duplicating the bookmark:

1. Click the arrow tool in the tool bar.
2. Hold the shift key on your keyboard.
3. Click the image and then click each text box. (Be sure to continue to hold the shift key. This will allow you to select more than one object.)
4. Let go of the shift key.
5. Pull down the **Edit** menu to **Copy**.
6. Pull down the **Edit** menu to **Paste**.
7. Carefully click and drag the center of the image to the next bookmark location.
8. Repeat steps 6 and 7 to create four bookmarks.
9. SAVE!

Printing and cutting:

1. Print.
2. Trim 1/2 inch from top, bottom, and sides.
3. Cut apart to create 4 bookmarks.
4. If you want, punch a hole in the top and add a yarn or a ribbon.

Candy "Rappers"

Grade Level:
K
1
2
• 3
• 4
• 5
• 6

Content Area:
Math
• Language Arts
Social Studies
• Science
• Cross Curricular

Multiple Intelligences:
• Verbal / Linguistic
Logical / Mathematical
Spatial
• Bodily / Kinesthetic
• Musical
Interpersonal
Intrapersonal
Naturalist

CD-ROM Templates:
• 08candy.doc - Microsoft Word
• 08candy.cwk - AppleWorks

Overview:
In this activity, students will write a poem or rap about candy or chocolate and put it on a candy bar wrapper. Then they will create a "chocolate bar" using cardboard and foil and cover it with their wrapper.

Software:
Microsoft Word or AppleWorks Drawing

ISTE Standards:
• Students develop positive attitudes toward technology uses that support lifelong learning, collaboration, personal pursuits, and productivity.
• Students use technology tools to enhance learning, increase productivity, and promote creativity.

Web Resources:
Mysteries of Chocolate - http://faculty.washington.edu/chudler/choco.html
Candy USA - http://www.candyusa.org/
All About Chocolate - http://www.fmnh.org/Chocolate/kids.html

The Teacher's Role:
1. The teacher will assist the students as they write short poems or raps about chocolate or candy.
2. The teacher will show the students how to design their wrapper and add their poem.
3. The teacher will provide aluminum foil, cardboard, and glue or tape.
3. The teacher will demonstrate how to create the cardboard candy bar and cover it with their wrapper.

Student Instructions:

Creating the Wrapper:

1. Open an AppleWorks Draw or Microsoft Word document.
2. Click to select the rectangle tool.
3. Drag a rectangle that is 5 inches wide and 6 inches long.
4. Use the Text tool to add a text box. The text box should be 4 inches wide and 2 inches long.
5. Enter your poem or rap in the text box.
6. Add your name.
7. Change the fonts, sizes, colors, and alignment.
8. Move and resize the text box so that it is centered within the rectangle.
9. SAVE! Print and cut around the rectangle.

Creating the Candy Bar:

1. Cut a piece of cardboard 2 1/2 x 5 1/2 inches.
2. Cover the cardboard with foil.
3. Place your wrapper over the "candy bar", making sure the poem is centered on the front.
4. Fold the wrapper around the "candy bar" and tape or glue to hold it together on the back.

Extensions:

• Students can work in pairs or groups to complete the activity.
• Instead of writing poems or raps, students could write facts about candy or chocolate.
   OR
• Students could write a poem or rap that *includes* a fact about candy or chocolate.
• Hang the students' creations on a bulletin board or in a hallway!

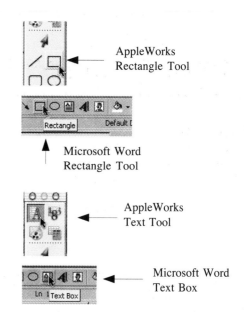

AppleWorks
Rectangle Tool

Microsoft Word
Rectangle Tool

AppleWorks
Text Tool

Microsoft Word
Text Box

Appleworks

Microsoft Word

Chocolate, chocolate
I declare
I don't know what I'd do
If you weren't there!
by Tammy

Chocolate is yummy
Chocolate is sweet.
Chocolate is tasty
and fun to eat!
by Todd

Famous Person Fact Flipper

Grade Level:
- K (See extensions)
- 1 (See extensions)
- 2
- 3
- 4
- 5
- 6

Content Area:
- Math
- Language Arts
- Social Studies
- Science
- Cross Curricular

Multiple Intelligences:
- Verbal / Linguistic
- Logical / Mathematical
- Spatial
- Bodily / Kinesthetic
- Musical
- Interpersonal
  Intrapersonal
- Naturalist

CD-ROM Templates:
• 09flipper.ppt - Microsoft PowerPoint

Overview:
In this activity, students create 6 question slides and 6 answer slides using PowerPoint Then they print the slides 6 per page. Students cut around the question slides (page 1) on 3 sides and then glue page one on top of page 2. Viewers lift the question to see the answer.

Software:
Microsoft PowerPoint

ISTE Standards:
• Students use a variety of media and formats to communicate information and ideas effectively to multiple audiences.
• Students use technology tools to enhance learning, increase productivity, and promote creativity.

Web Resources:
Yahooligans - www.yahooligans.com
KidsClick - www.kidsclick.org
Enchanted Learning - www.enchantedlearning.com

The Teacher's Role:
1. The teacher will help the students choose a famous person.
2. The teacher will demonstrate how to use a search tool or other web site to find information about the person. (If time is limited, you may want to use books for resources.)
3. The teacher shows the students how to create the 12 slides (see student instructions.)
4. The teacher demonstrates how to print and cut to create the fact flipper.

Student Instructions:
Basic PowerPoint Instructions:
Adding Text:
1. Click to select the text box tool.
2. Click and drag to create a text box on the slide.
3. Type your text.
4. Change the fonts and sizes if you want.

Adding Word Art
1. Click to select the word art tool.
2. Choose a word art style.
3. Type your words; click OK.
4. Click and drag the center of the word art to move it.
5. Click and drag a "handle point" of the word art to resize it.

Adding Images
1. Paste an image that has been copied from the Internet or another source.
or
1. Pull down the **Insert** menu to **Picture** and pull over to **Clip Art**.
2. Choose an image from the provided clip gallery.

Choosing a person:
1. Choose a famous person.
2. Find 5 facts about that person using books, the Internet, or other resources.

Creating the fact flipper:
1. Open a new blank PowerPoint document.
2. Add text and images to 12 slides:

Slide 1	Add a title and the instructions.
Slide 2-6	Enter a question on each of the slides.
Slide 7	Enter your name, class, and date.
Slide 8-12	Enter the answers to the questions from slides 2-6.

3. SAVE!
4. Print as a handout 6 slides per page.
   Page 1 will contain your title and questions; Page 2 will contain your name and your answers.
5. On page 1, cut around both sides and the bottom of each slide to create a "flap".
6. Put glue on the back of page 1 -- do not put glue on the "flaps."
7. Place page 1 on top of page 2 so that the slides are directly on top of each other.

Extensions:
• Fact flippers can be created for any content area or topic: math facts, story problems, places, animals, vocabulary words and definitions, music terms, true - false questions, etc.
• **Young students** could create a fact flipper for beginning sounds, numbers, or shapes.
• Fact flippers make a nice hallway display. You may want to mount them onto heavier paper first. Add a sign or caption that says, "You'll FLIP Over These Facts!"

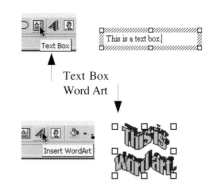

Text Box
Word Art

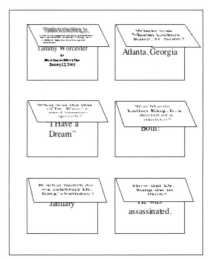

▲ Page 1 - Cut on dotted lines to create "flaps".

▲ Glue page 1 on top of Page 2. Viewers lift "flaps to view answers!

Picture Post Cards

Grade Level:
K
1
- 2
- 3
- 4
- 5
- 6

Content Area:
Math
- Language Arts
- Social Studies
Science
- Cross Curricular

Multiple Intelligences:
- Verbal / Linguistic
  Logical / Mathematical
- Spatial
  Bodily / Kinesthetic
  Musical
- Interpersonal
  Intrapersonal
- Naturalist

CD-ROM Templates:
- 10postcard.ppt - Microsoft PowerPoint
- 10postcard.cwk - AppleWorks

Overview:
In this activity, students will design a post card with a picture and a few facts about a place they've "visited."

Software:
AppleWorks Drawing Program or Microsoft PowerPoint

ISTE Standards:
- Students are proficient in the use of technology.
- Students use technology tools to enhance learning, increase productivity, and promote creativity.
- Students use technology to locate, evaluate, and collect information from a variety of sources.

Web Resources:
- Pics 4 Learning - http://www.pics4learning.com/
- The Amazing Picture Machine - http://www.ncrtec.org/picture.htm

The Teacher's Role:
1. The teacher will assist the students or teams in choosing a place to visit (a virtual visit, of course!) OR
2. The teacher will assign a place to each student or team.
3. The teacher will demonstrate how to find a picture on the Internet and how to copy and paste it.
4. The teacher will demonstrate how to create a rectangle and how to add pictures and text to the document.

Student Instructions:

Copying the Picture

1. Open your browser (Internet Explorer or Netscape) and go to a site such as:
   - Pics 4 Learning - http://www.pics4learning.com/
   - The Amazing Picture Machine - http://www.ncrtec.org/picture.htm
2. Search to find a picture of your "place."
3. Position your cursor directly over the image.
4. On a *Macintosh* computer, click and hold the mouse button (or control-click).
   On a *Windows* computer, click the right mouse button. A menu should appear.
5. Choose "Copy Image" or "Copy."

Creating the Picture PostCard

1. Open an AppleWorks Drawing document or a blank PowerPoint slide.
2. Use the Rectangle tool to create the postcard outline.
3. Pull down the **Edit** menu to **Paste**. (This will paste the image that you copied earlier from the Internet.)
4. Move and resize your image so that it fits on the left half of your postcard.

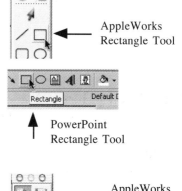

AppleWorks
Rectangle Tool

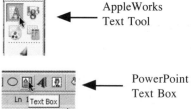

PowerPoint
Rectangle Tool

Adding Text

1. Click to select the text tool (AppleWorks) or the text box (PowerPoint).
2. Click and drag to create a "box" on the right half of your postcard. (Be sure to leave room for the stamp at the top!)
3. Enter the greeting, body, closing, and signature of your message.
   IMPORTANT -- Be sure to include at least three facts about your place!
4. Change the fonts, sizes, colors, etc. if you want.
5. SAVE, print, and cut! (You may want to print onto heavy paper.)

AppleWorks
Text Tool

PowerPoint
Text Box

Note - In PowerPoint, you may want to print as a handout - 2 per page.

Student Challenge!

1. Use the drawing tools or clip art to add a stamp to the upper right corner.

Dear Mom and Dad,

Today we went to Stonehenge, in southern England. It was really cool! I didn't know that it took over 1400 years to build it! I can see why it is one of the world's greatest mysteries. I can't believe it was built by HAND without the use of modern machinery.

Wish you were here!

Love,
Tammy

State Mini-Books

Grade Level:
- K
- 1
- 2
- 3
- 4
- 5
- 6

Content Area:
- Math
- Language Arts
- Social Studies
- Science
- Cross Curricular

Multiple Intelligences:
- Verbal / Linguistic
- Logical / Mathematical
- Spatial
- Bodily / Kinesthetic
- Musical
- Interpersonal
- Intrapersonal
- Naturalist

CD-ROM Templates:
- 11minibook.ppt - Microsoft PowerPoint

Overview:
In this activity, students create and print mini-books about a chosen state.

Software:
Microsoft PowerPoint

ISTE Standards:
- Use keyboards and other common input and output devices efficiently and effectively.
- Use technology tools for individual and collaborative writing, communication, and publishing activities.

Web Resources:
50 States.com - http://www.50states.com/

The Teacher's Role:
1. The teacher will introduce the students to the 50 States web site.
2. The teacher will demonstrate how to copy and paste text and pictures from the Internet.
3. The teacher will show how to create slides in PowerPoint.
4. The teacher will demonstrate how to print the slides 6-per-page.
5. The teacher will show students how to cut and staple their mini-books.

Student Instructions:

General Instructions:
To copy and paste text from the Internet:
1. Click and drag to select the text you want to copy.
2. Pull down the **Edit** menu to **Copy**.
3. Move to your PowerPoint slide.
4. Pull down the **Edit** menu to **Paste**.

To copy and paste an image from the Internet:
1. Find an Internet image you want to use.
2. Position your cursor directly over the image.
3. On a *Macintosh* computer, click and hold the mouse button (or control-click).
   On a *Windows* computer, click the right mouse button. A menu should appear.
4. Choose "Copy Image" or "Copy."
5. Move to your PowerPoint slide.
6. Pull down the **Edit** menu to **Paste**.

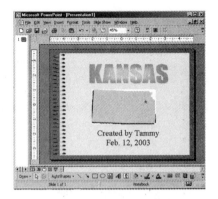

Slide 1:
1. Choose a state. Browse to find information about your state on the Internet. (You may want to try www.50states.com.)
2. Open a new PowerPoint document.
3. Choose a blank slide show, or choose a design template that you like.
4. Enter the name of your chosen state. (Use the Text tool or Word Art.)
5. Copy a picture of your state from the Internet and paste it onto your slide.
6. Enter your name and the date.

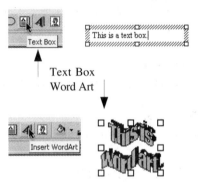

Text Box
Word Art

Slides 2-6:
1. Pull down the **Insert** menu to **New Slide**.
2. Add text and images to your slide with information about your state. You may want to add information about the state's capital, population, flower, flag, etc.
3. Repeat steps 1 and 2 for each slide.
4. SAVE!

Creating the Mini-Book
1. Pull down the **File** menu to **Print**.
2. In the PowerPoint print options, choose to print handouts at 6 per page.
3. Print.
4. Cut around slides, adding 1/2 inch to the left side of each.
   Note - Look at the dotted lines at the right to see where to cut.
5. Staple the slides together to create a mini-book!

Extensions:
- Students can create mini books for any topic: persons, places, animals, things, etc.
- Students could write their own story and then turn it into a mini-book.
- Students could create an "all about me" mini-book.

Staple slides together to create a mini-book.

I'm T-rrific!

Grade Level:
- K (with help)
- 1 (with help)
- 2
- 3
- 4
- 5
- 6

Content Area:
Math
- Language Arts
Social Studies
Science
- Cross Curricular

Multiple Intelligences:
- Verbal / Linguistic
Logical / Mathematical
- Spatial
- Bodily / Kinesthetic
Musical
Interpersonal
- Intrapersonal
Naturalist

CD-ROM Templates:
- 12tshirt.ppt - Microsoft PowerPoint
- 12tshirt.cwk - AppleWorks

Overview:
In this activity, students will design and print T-shirts that tell why they are T-rrific!

Software:
Microsoft PowerPoint or AppleWorks Drawing

ISTE Standards:
- Students develop positive attitudes toward technology uses that support lifelong learning, collaboration, personal pursuits, and productivity.
- Students use technology tools to enhance learning, increase productivity, and promote creativity.

The Teacher's Role:
1. The teacher will assist the students as they write down ways they are terrific.
2. The teacher will show the students how to enter their text in a PowerPoint or AppleWorks Drawing document.
3. The teacher will show the students how to fold and cut their T-shirts.

Student Instructions:

AppleWorks Drawing:
1. Open an AppleWorks Drawing document.
2. Click to select the text tool.
3. Click and drag to create a text box.
4. Type the text, "I'm T-rrific because:".
5. Press the Return / Enter key on your keyboard.
6. Enter 4 or 5 reasons you are terrific, pressing the Return / Enter key after each reason.
7. Change the fonts, sizes, and colors and alignments if you want.
8. Select the arrow tool and click and drag the text box to the center of the page. Click and drag a corner square to resize the text box.
   (Make sure you leave about 3 inches of space above the text and about 2 inches on each side of the text.)
9. SAVE and print.

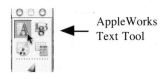

AppleWorks Text Tool

Microsoft PowerPoint:
1. Open a blank Microsoft PowerPoint document.
2. Pull down the **File** menu to **Page Setup**.
3. Choose the Portrait orientation.
4. Click the WordArt tool and type the text, "I'm T-rrific because:".
5. Click and drag the word art to the center of the page about 3 inches down from the top. Click and drag a corner square to resize the text.
6. Choose the Text Box tool and click and drag to create a text box below the title.
7. Type 4 or 5 reasons you're terrific, pressing the Enter or Return key after each reason.
8. Click and drag the edge of the text box to move it to the center of the page. Click and drag a corner square to resize the text box.
   (Make sure you leave about 2 inches of space on each side of the text box.)
9. SAVE and print.

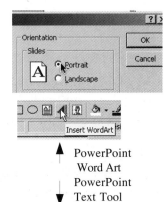

PowerPoint Word Art

PowerPoint Text Tool

Cutting the T-shirt:

1. Fold in half.　　2. Cut as shown above.　　3. Unfold to create a T-shirt!

I'm T-rrific because:

I can play the piano!

I help with my baby brother!

I get good grades!

I am nice to other people!

I feed my dog every day!

Extensions:
• Students can add their names to the bottom of the shirt.
• Use miniature clothespins to hang the shirts on a "clothesline" in the hallway or on a bulletin board.

Weather Acrostics

Grade Level:
- K (See extensions)
- 1 (See extensions)
- 2
- 3
- 4
- 5
- 6

Content Area:
Math
- Language Arts
  Social Studies
- Science
- Cross Curricular

Multiple Intelligences:
- Verbal / Linguistic
  Logical / Mathematical
- Spatial
  Bodily / Kinesthetic
  Musical
  Interpersonal
- Intrapersonal
- Naturalist

CD-ROM Templates:
- 13acrostic.ppt - Microsoft PowerPoint
- 13acrostic.cwk - AppleWorks

Overview:
In this activity, students will choose a weather term and will type it vertically on the page. Then they will add facts or descriptors that begin with each letter in the term.

Software:
Microsoft PowerPoint, or
AppleWorks Drawing

ISTE Standards:
- Students are proficient in the use of technology.
- Students use technology tools to enhance learning, increase productivity, and promote creativity.
- Students use technology to locate, evaluate, and collect information from a variety of sources.

Web Resources:
NSSL's Weather Room - http://www.nssl.noaa.gov/edu/
Dan's Wild Weather Page - http://www.wildwildweather.com/
Meteorology A-Z - http://www.wxdude.com/topics.html

The Teacher's Role:
1. The teacher will provide books, articles, and web resources about weather.
2. The teacher will demonstrate how to add vertical text.
3. The teacher will demonstrate how to add text boxes for the facts / descriptors.
4. The teacher will show students how to add clip art.

Student Instructions:

Entering Vertical Text

AppleWorks:
1. Open an AppleWorks Drawing Document.
2. Use the text tool to add a text box to the page.
3. Type your weather word in all capital letters. Be sure to press the Return key on your keyboard after each letter.
4. With the Arrow tool selected, click and drag the text box to the left side of the page.
5. Make the font size larger.

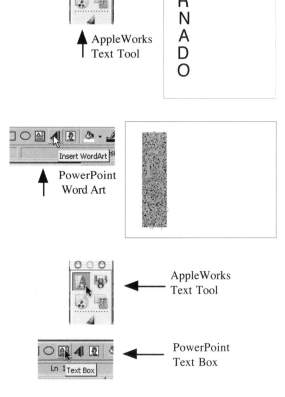

▲ AppleWorks
  Text Tool

PowerPoint:
1. Open a blank PowerPoint slide.
2. Click the Word Art tool.
3. In the Word Art window, choose a vertical text option.
4. Click and drag the center of the word to move the word art to the left side of the screen.
5. Click and drag a handle point to make the word art larger.

▲ PowerPoint
  Word Art

Adding Facts / Descriptors:
1. Click to select the text tool (AppleWorks) or the text box (PowerPoint).
2. Click and drag to create a "box" beside the top letter of your weather word.
3. Enter a fact or describing word that begins with that letter.
4. Repeat steps 2 and 3 for each letter of the vertical word.
5. Change the font, sizes, and colors if you want.
7. Add an appropriate clip art:
   - AppleWorks - Pull down the **File** menu to **Show Clippings** (or **Library**).
   - PowerPoint - Pull down the **Insert** menu to **Picture** and pull over to **Clip Art**.
6. SAVE and print.

← AppleWorks
  Text Tool

← PowerPoint
  Text Box

Extensions:
- Students could create acrostics for any subject (person, place, event, animal, etc.)
- Students could create an acrostic about themselves by placing their name at the side and adding characteristics that begin with each letter.

- **For Younger Students:**
- Kindergarten and 1st grade students can use the Kid Pix program to create acrostics:
   a. Add a vertical word to the left side of the screen.
   b. Use the rubber stamp tool or character tools to add pictures that begin with each letter of the word.

S wirling!
N o school!
O utdoor fun!
W inter Wonderla

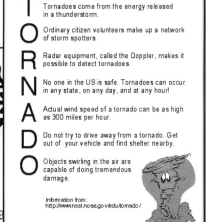

T Tornadoes come from the energy released in a thunderstorm.
O Ordinary citizen volunteers make up a network of storm spotters.
R Radar equipment, called the Doppler, makes it possible to detect tornadoes.
N No one in the US is safe. Tornadoes can occur in any state, on any day, and at any hour!
A Actual wind speed of a tornado can be as high as 300 miles per hour.
D Do not try to drive away from a tornado. Get out of your vehicle and find shelter nearby.
O Objects swirling in the air are capable of doing tremendous damage.

Information from:
http://www.nssl.noaa.gov/edu/tornado /

Zip-Up Leaf Displays

Grade Level:
- K (see extensions)
- 1 (see extensions)
- 2
- 3
- 4
- 5
- 6

Content Area:
- Math
- Language Arts
  Social Studies
- Science
- Cross Curricular

Multiple Intelligences:
- Verbal / Linguistic
- Logical / Mathematical
- Spatial
- Bodily / Kinesthetic
  Musical
  Interpersonal
  Intrapersonal
- Naturalist

CD-ROM Templates:
- 14zip.ppt - Microsoft PowerPoint
- 14zip.cwk - AppleWorks

Overview:
In this activity, students collect leaves from different trees and put them into sandwich sized zip lock bags. Students then create a "bag tag" to display the name of and information about the leaf.

Software:
Microsoft Word or AppleWorks Drawing

ISTE Standards:
- Use keyboards and other common input and output devices efficiently and effectively.
- Students use technology tools to enhance learning, increase productivity, and promote creativity.

Web Resources:
What Tree Is It? - http://www.oplin.lib.oh.us/products/tree/index.html
Trees and Leaves Photo Guide - http://www.watersheds.org/nature/treeguide.htm

The Teacher's Role:
1. The teacher will provide the students with tree identification books and/or Web sites.
2. The teacher will assist the students in collecting a variety of leaves.
3. The teacher will provide sandwich size zip lock bags. (Or ask students to bring their own.)
4. The teacher will demonstrate how to create the "bag tag".
5. The teacher will show the students how to print, fold, and attach the bag tag.

Student Instructions:

Collecting the leaves:

1. Collect leaves from a variety of different trees.
2. Choose one leaf to display. (Your teacher may assign one to you.)
3. Put your leaf inside a sandwich sized zip lock bag.
4. Use books or web resources to learn what kind of leaf it is.
5. Find out a few facts about your leaf and the tree it came from.

Creating the bag tags:

1. Open a Microsoft Word or AppleWorks Drawing document.
2. If the rulers aren't showing, turn them on:
   AppleWorks - Pull down the **Format** menu to **Rulers** and pull over to **Show Rulers**.
   Microsoft Word - Pull down the **View** menu to **Ruler**.
3. Set the top and bottom margins at 0.
4. Set the left and right margins at .5.
   Note - If you get a warning message, click **Ignore**.
5. Pretend that the page is divided equally into 4 horizontal sections. Your text will go in section 3. (See image at right.)
6. Add a text box to section three. (Make sure you place it between the 5 1/2" and the 8 1/4" marks on the ruler.)
7. Enter the name of your leaf and some information about it.
8. Change the fonts and sizes if you want.
9. SAVE!

Putting it together:

1. Print the bag tag on a full sheet of paper.
2. Fold the paper in half (so that you can see your text).
3. Open the page and fold both ends into the center.
4. Put the folded bag tag over the top of your zip lock bag.
5. Staple the tag to the bag!

Extensions:

• Students could be challenged to add to their leaf collection throughout the year. If students travel during the year, leaves from different states / countries could be added.
• Students can use the "bag tag" idea to display collections of rocks, sea shells, fossils, seeds, soil samples, insects, etc.
• Students could put a seed inside the bag with a wet paper towel to create a sprout display. The label could show the name of seed.
• Students could create a clay model of a blood cell and display it with a bag tag.

• **Young students** could label the bag tags with the names of shapes and then display things that are circles, squares, etc.
   Or -- label the bag with a number and then put that number of objects in the bag.
   Or --label with a letter and add objects that begin with that letter...

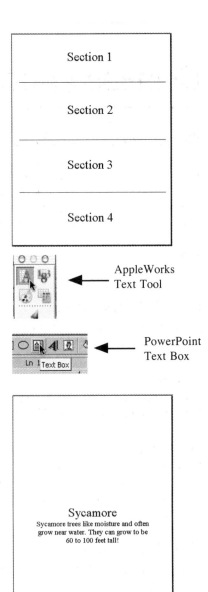

AppleWorks Text Tool

PowerPoint Text Box

Sycamore
Sycamore trees like moisture and often grow near water. They can grow to be 60 to 100 feet tall!

Sycamore
Sycamore trees like moisture and often grow near water. They can grow to be 60 to 100 feet tall!

Chinese Lantern

Grade Level:
- K
- 1
- 2
- 3
- 4
- 5
- 6

Content Area:
Math
Language Arts
- Social Studies
Science
- Cross Curricular

Multiple Intelligences:
Verbal / Linguistic
- Logical / Mathematical
- Spatial
Bodily / Kinesthetic
Musical
- Interpersonal
Intrapersonal
Naturalist

CD-ROM Templates:
- 15lantern.doc - Microsoft Word
- 15lantern.cwk - AppleWorks

Overview:
In this activity, students will use a painting or drawing program to create a design and print on a full sheet of paper. Then they will cut and fold to create a Chinese lantern.

Software:
Windows - Paint (Start -- Programs -- Accessories -- Paint); KidPix; PowerPoint
Macintosh - AppleWorks Paint or Draw; Kid Pix; or other paint/draw program
NOTE - Any program that provides drawing tools and prints on a full sheet of paper will do!

ISTE Standards:
- Students use technology tools to enhance learning, increase productivity, and promote creativity.
- Students develop positive attitudes toward technology uses that support lifelong learning, collaboration, personal pursuits, and productivity.

Web Resources:
My Web 3000 - http://www.myweb3000.com/Lantern.html
Chinese New Year - http://www.kidsdomain.com/holiday/chineseny.html

The Teacher's Role:
1. The teacher will provide resources about the Chinese New Year and the significance of the lantern.
2. The teacher will demonstrate how to use a painting or drawing program to add colors and designs so that it will print on a full sheet of paper.
3. The teacher will provide an example and will show students how to fold, cut, and finish their lanterns.

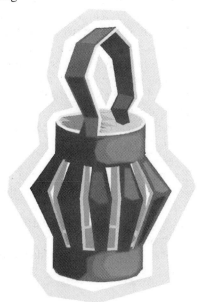

Student Instructions:

On the computer:

1. Open a painting or drawing program.
2. Turn the page so that it will print sideways (horizontal). In most programs you'll find this option by pulling down the **File** menu to **Page Setup**.
3. Use the drawing tools to add a design to the page.
4. Add clip art and text if you want!
5. SAVE and Print.
6. If your printer doesn't print in color, you may want to print onto colored paper and/or use markers or crayons to color your picture.

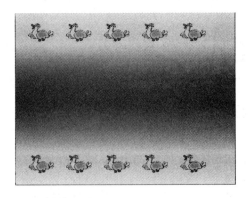

Creating the lantern:

1. Fold the page in half (like a hot dog bun).
2. Use your scissors to cut slits about every 2 inches. Do NOT cut all the way through - stop about an inch before the top!
3. Carefully open the page.
4. Hold the page at the top with one hand on each side.
5. Curl the top corners towards each other to form a circle (the lantern top).
6. Use tape, glue, or a staple to hold the corners together.
7. Repeat with the bottom.
8. Add a handle.
9. Hang from the ceiling or doorways.

Cutting lines

Extensions:

• To conserve printer ink, students could create miniature lanterns. Follow the same instructions, but just create on a smaller scale.
• Students could type a poem on their lantern before printing it.
• Before creating the lanterns, students could compare American and Chinese New Year celebration customs.

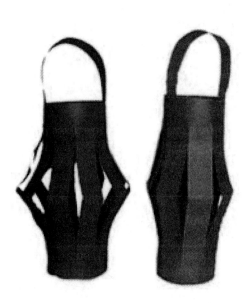

Create Your Own Animal!

Grade Level:
- K
- 1
- • 2
- • 3
- • 4
- • 5
- • 6

Content Area:
- Math
- • Language Arts
- Social Studies
- • Science
- • Cross Curricular

Multiple Intelligences:
- • Verbal / Linguistic
- • Logical / Mathematical
- • Spatial
- Bodily / Kinesthetic
- Musical
- Interpersonal
- Intrapersonal
- • Naturalist

CD-ROM Templates:
- • 16animal.bmp - Windows Paint
- • 16animal.cwk - AppleWorks

Overview:
In this activity, students will use the painting tools to put different animal parts together to create their own animal. Then they will give it a name and write a paragraph or story about it.

Software:
Windows - Paint (Start -- Programs -- Accessories -- Paint)
Macintosh - AppleWorks Paint

ISTE Standards:
- • Students are proficient in the use of technology.
- • Students use technology tools to enhance learning, increase productivity, and promote creativity.

Web Resources:
- • Enchanted Learning Animal Printouts - http://www.EnchantedLearning.com/coloring/

The Teacher's Role:
1. The teacher will explain the "create your own" animal activity.
2. The teacher will demonstrate how to copy an animal picture from the Internet and paste it into a painting program.
3. The teacher will show how to use the lasso to select a part (such as the head) of an animal and paste it into a second painting window.
4. The teacher will instruct the students to give their animal a name and write a paragraph or story about their new creation (optional).

Student Instructions:

Getting Ready:
1. Open a paint program.
2. Save the blank screen as "working".
3. Open a new paint window. (Pull down the **File** menu to **New**.)
4. Save the new blank screen as "newanimal".

Note - You will use the "working" document to select the animal parts. You will use the "newanimal" document to assemble your new animal.

"Capturing" an Animal:
1. Browse the animal pictures at http://www.EnchantedLearning.com/coloring/ to find two or three animals you want to use.
2. Choose and open the picture of one animal.
3. Position your cursor directly over the image.
4. On a *Macintosh* computer, click and hold the mouse button (or control-click). On a *Windows* computer, click the right mouse button. A menu should appear.
5. Choose "Copy Image" or "Copy".

Creating a New Animal:
1. Open your "working" paint document.
2. Pull down the **Edit** menu to **Paste**. (This will paste your animal onto the screen.)
3. Use one of the selector tools to select part of the animal (maybe the head).
4. Pull down the **Edit** menu to **Copy**.
5. Open your "newanimal" paint document.
6. Pull down the **Edit** menu to **Paste**.
7. Repeat steps 2-5 of "'Capturing' an Animal" and steps 1-6 of "Creating a New Animal" until your new animal is complete.
8. Use the paint tools to add details and colors to your animal.

AppleWorks Paint
Selector Tools

WIndows Paint
Selector Tools

Naming your Animal:
1. Combine the names of the original animals to create a name for your new animal.
2. Use the text tool to label the animal with its new name.
3. SAVE!

Extensions:
• Copy your new animal and paste it into a word processing document. Then write a paragraph or a story about your new animal. Be sure to include facts about where it lives, what it eats, how large it is, etc.

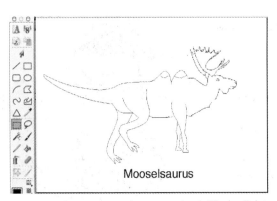

AppleWorks Paint

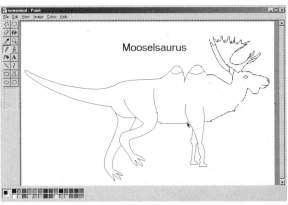

Windows - Paint

Draw Me!

Grade Level:
K
1
• 2
• 3
• 4
• 5
• 6

Content Area:
Math
• Language Arts
Social Studies
Science
• Cross Curricular

Multiple Intelligences:
• Verbal / Linguistic
Logical / Mathematical
• Spatial
• Bodily / Kinesthetic
Musical
Interpersonal
Intrapersonal
Naturalist

CD-ROM Templates:
• 17drawme.bmp - Windows Paint
• 17drawme.cwk - AppleWorks

Overview:
In this constructivist activity, students experiment with the tools of a Painting program to complete an activity from a "Learn to Draw" book or Web Page.

Software:
Windows - Paint (Start -- Programs -- Accessories -- Paint); HyperStudio; Kid Pix
Macintosh - AppleWorks Paint; HyperStudio; Kid Pix; or other paint program

ISTE Standards:
• Students are proficient in the use of technology.
• Students use technology tools to enhance learning, increase productivity, and promote creativity.

Web Resources:
Draw and Color with Uncle Fred - http://www.unclefred.com/
Billy Bear Learn to Draw - http://www.billybear4kids.com/Learn2Draw/L

The Teacher's Role:
1. The teacher will provide books or printouts from web sites with step-by-step "how to draw" instructions.
2. The teacher will show the students how to find and open a paint program on their computer.
3. The teacher will quickly show the tools and options. *(Note - since this is a student-discovery activity, the students will do most ot the exploring and learning on their own.)*

Student Instructions:

1. Open a Paint program on your computer.
2. Choose an activity from one of the books or handouts your teacher has given you.
3. Experiment with the tools and options to complete the "draw-me" activity on your computer.
4. Be ready to pull down the **Edit** menu to **Undo** if you make a mistake!
5. SAVE!
6. Print.

Student Challenges:

• Which works better for freehand drawing -- the pencil tool or the paint brush tool? Why?
• How do you make the lines thicker? Thinner?
• Can you move an object once you've placed it on the screen? If so, how?

Extensions:

• Instead of using "Draw-me" resources, use coloring books and have the students try to replicate the pictures.
• Students could write a story about their finished picture.
• Older students could create their own set of step-by-step "draw me" instructions.

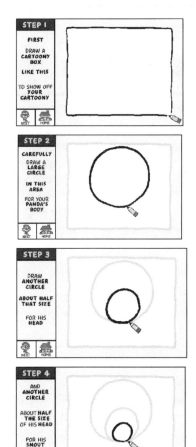

Example Instructions from
www.unclefred.com

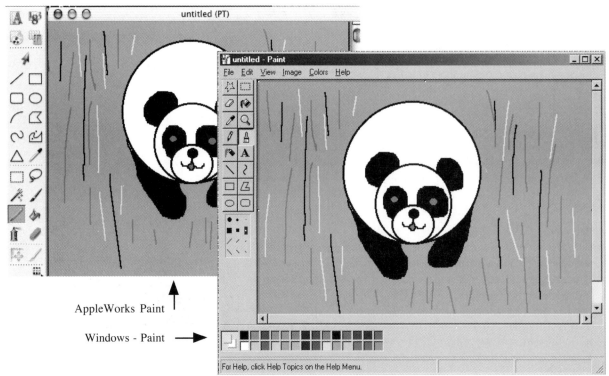

AppleWorks Paint

Windows - Paint ➔

Following Directions

Grade Level:
- K
- 1
- 2
- 3
- 4
- 5
- 6

Content Area:
Math
- Language Arts
- Social Studies
Science
- Cross Curricular

Multiple Intelligences:
- Verbal / Linguistic
- Logical / Mathematical
- Spatial
Bodily / Kinesthetic
Musical
- Interpersonal
Intrapersonal
Naturalist

Overview:
In this activity, one student will give directions for adding things to a paint / draw document. (example: Put a small blue square in the upper right corner. Type your name in the center of the screen.) Other students will follow the directions as best they can. When they are done, the students will compare their pictures to see how well they presented and/or followed directions.

Software:
Windows - Paint (Start -- Programs -- Accessories -- Paint); HyperStudio; KidPix
Macintosh - AppleWorks Painting or Drawing; HyperStudio; Kid Pix; or other paint program

ISTE Standards:
- Students are proficient in the use of technology.
- Students use technology tools to enhance learning, increase productivity, and promote creativity.

The Teacher's Role:
1. The teacher will explain the activity to the students.
2. The teacher will give a brief overview of how to use the drawing / painting tools to add shapes, colors, and text to the document.
3. The teacher will model the activity.
4. The teacher will choose a student to be the next instruction "giver."

Student Instructions:

1. Open a paint or drawing program.
2. Your teacher will choose one student to be the SPEAKER. The remaining students will be the LISTENERS.

The Speaker's Job:

1. The speaker will give 5 different directions to the listeners. Example directions:
   "Draw a small blue square in the upper left corner."
   "Type your name in the center of the screen."
   "Draw a line from the upper right corner to the lower left corner of the screen."
   "Draw a small red circle in the lower right corner."
   "Draw a line across the width of the page below the blue square."
2. The speaker will draw on his/her own screen as he/she gives directions.
3. When finished, the speaker will show his/her screen to the other students so they can compare.

   NOTE -- A projector or large screen display works great for this activity. Shut off the projector during the instructions and then turn it on so students can compare their drawings.

The Listener's Job:

1. The listener will carefully follow the speaker's instructions.
2. The listener cannot ask questions.
3. When finished, the listener will compare his/her drawing with the speaker's.

Extensions:

• Students can work in pairs with one being the speaker and one being the listener. They can take turns giving directions to each other and comparing screens.

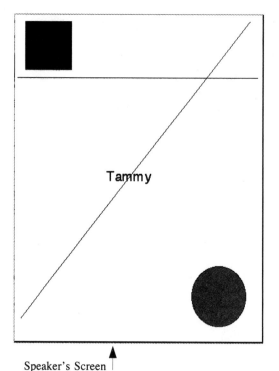

Tammy

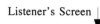

Speaker's Screen

Listener's Screen

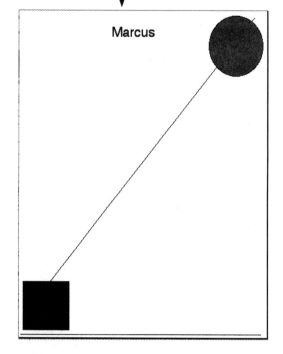

Marcus

Shape Poem

Grade Level:
- K
- 1
- 2
- 3
- 4
- 5
- 6

Content Area:
  Math
- Language Arts
  Social Studies
  Science
- Cross Curricular

Multiple Intelligences:
- Verbal / Linguistic
  Logical / Mathematical
- Spatial
  Bodily / Kinesthetic
  Musical
  Interpersonal
  Intrapersonal
  Naturalist

CD-ROM Templates:
- 19shapepoem - Kid Pix

Overview:
In this activity, students will create a shape made of text characters.

Software:
Kid Pix

ISTE Standards:
- Students use technology tools to enhance learning, increase productivity, and promote creativity.
- Students develop positive attitudes toward technology uses that support lifelong learning, collaboration, personal pursuits, and productivity.

The Teacher's Role:
1. The teacher will demonstrate how to open the Kid Pix program.
2. The teacher will demonstrate how to set the Alphabet Text option.
3. The teacher will demonstrate how to draw the outline of a shape using the alphabet text.

Student Instructions:

Kid Pix Studio Deluxe:

1. Open the Kid Pix painting program.
2. Choose what shape you want to draw. (house, flower, fish, snake, etc.)
3. Pull down the **Toolbox** (or Goodies) menu to **Alphabet Text**.
4. Type the letters to spell what you want to draw.
5. Click OK.
6. Choose the "Wacky Brush" tool and the "ABC" option.
7. Click and drag to draw your shape. (Note - for best results, drag from left to right.)
8. Use the other tools to add details to your shape.
9. SAVE!

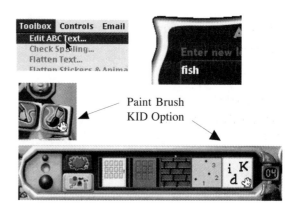

Wacky Brush
ABC Option

Kid Pix Deluxe 3:

1. Choose what shape you want to draw. (house, flower, fish, snake, etc.)
2. Click at the top of the screen to activate the menu bar.
3. Pull down the **Toolbox** menu to **Edit ABC Text**.
4. Type the letters to spell what you want to draw.
5. Click OK.
6. Choose the "Paint Brush" tool and the "KID" option.
7. Click and drag to draw your shape. (Note - for best results, drag from left to right.)
8. Use the other tools to add details to your shape.
9. SAVE!

Paint Brush
KID Option

Extensions:

• Students could draw parts of an object using different words:
  Stem; leaf; petal.
  House; door; window
• The teacher may want to provide children's coloring books to give students ideas of simple shapes to draw.
• Students can print their pictures and hang them in the hallway -- or all of the students' shape poems could be bound together into a book.

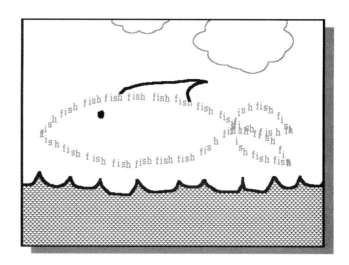

Daily Temperature Chart

Grade Level:

K
1
• 2
• 3
• 4
• 5
• 6

Content Area:

• Math
  Language Arts
  Social Studies
• Science
• Cross Curricular

Multiple Intelligences:

  Verbal / Linguistic
• Logical / Mathematical
• Spatial
  Bodily / Kinesthetic
  Musical
  Interpersonal
  Intrapersonal
• Naturalist

CD-ROM Templates:

• 20temperature.xls - Microsoft Excel
• 20temperature.cwk - AppleWorks

Overview:

In this activity, students will use a spreadsheet to chart the daily temperatures for a week.

Software:

Microsoft Excel or AppleWorks Spreadsheet

ISTE Standards:

• Students use technology to locate, evaluate, and collect information from a variety of sources.
• Students use technology tools to process data and report results.

Web Resources:

The Weather Channel - http://www.weather.com
Local TV Channels

The Teacher's Role:

1. The teacher will help the students record the high temperatures each day for a week.
2. The teacher will show students how to enter the data in a spreadsheet.
3. The teacher will demonstrate how to turn their data into a line graph.

Note -- If the students are not familiar with the spreadsheet, you may want to refer to the information at the bottom of page 43.

Student Instructions:

Entering the Data:

1. Open a new Microsoft Excel or AppleWorks Spreadsheet document.
2. Enter the labels, "Day," "High," and "Low" in cells A1, B1, and C1.
3. Enter the days of the week in column A.
4. Enter the high and low temperatures in columns B and C.

	A	B	C
1	Day	High	Low
2	Monday	60	45
3	Tuesday	72	60
4	Wednesday	80	55
5	Thursday	73	57
6	Friday	65	58
7			

Creating the Chart:

Excel:

1. Click and drag to select all cells that have information in them.
   NOTE - do not select any blank cells!
2. Pull down the **Insert** menu to **Chart**.
3. Choose the Line chart with markers.
4. Click the Next button twice to get to Step 3.
5. Enter the title, "Daily Temperatures".
6. Click Finish.
7. SAVE!

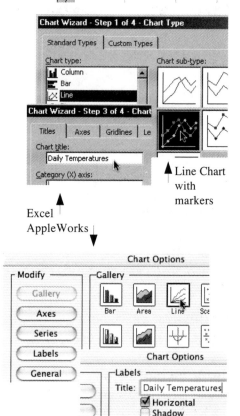

Appleworks:

1. Click and drag to select all cells that have information in them.
   NOTE - do not select any blank cells!
2. Pull down the **Options** menu to **Make Chart**.
3. Choose the Line option.
4. Click the Label button.
5. Enter the title, "Daily Temperatures".
6. Click OK.
7. SAVE!

Student Challenges:

(Use the help menu if necessary)
• Can you change the colors of the lines?
• Can you label the x and y axis?
• Can you change the color of the background of the chart?

Extensions:

• Students could work in pairs or teams to complete the activity.
• Students could chart the temperatures for an entire month.

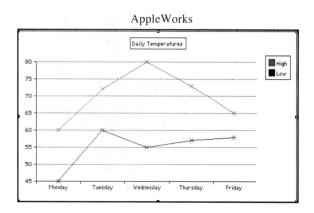

AppleWorks

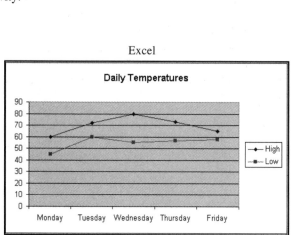

Excel

Eye Color Bar Chart

Grade Level:
- K
- 1
- • 2
- • 3
- • 4
- • 5
- • 6

Content Area:
- • Math
- Language Arts
- • Social Studies
- Science
- • Cross Curricular

Multiple Intelligences:
- Verbal / Linguistic
- • Logical / Mathematical
- • Spatial
- Bodily / Kinesthetic
- Musical
- • Interpersonal
- Intrapersonal
- Naturalist

CD-ROM Templates:
- • 21eyecolor.xls - Microsoft Excel
- • 21eyecolor.cwk - AppleWorks

Overview:
In this activity, students will use a spreadsheet to create a bar graph that shows the class's eye colors.

Software:
Microsoft Excel or AppleWorks Spreadsheet

ISTE Standards:
- • Students use technology to locate, evaluate, and collect information from a variety of sources.
- • Students use technology tools to process data and report results.

The Teacher's Role:
1. The teacher will conduct a poll to find out the students' eye color. (Just name a color and have students raise their hands.)
2. The teacher will record the results and will post them where all students can see them. (ex. Blue - 9, Green - 4, Brown - 12, Hazel - 5, Gray - 1)
3. The teacher will demonstrate how to enter the data into a spreadsheet.
4. The teacher will show the students how to turn their data into a bar graph.

Note -- If the students are not familiar with the spreadsheet, you may want to refer to the information at the bottom of page 43.

Student Instructions:

Entering the Data:
1. Open a new Microsoft Excel or AppleWorks Spreadsheet document.
2. Enter the eye colors in column A.
3. Enter the numbers in column B.

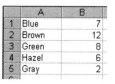

	A	B
1	Blue	7
2	Brown	12
3	Green	8
4	Hazel	6
5	Gray	2

Creating the Chart:
Excel:
1. Click and drag to select all cells that have information in them. NOTE - do not select any blank cells!
2. Pull down the **Insert** menu to **Chart**.
3. Choose the Column or Bar option. Click Next.
4. Click to change the series to Rows. Click Next
5. Enter the title, "Eye Color."
6. Click Finish; SAVE!

AppleWorks:
1. Click and drag to select all cells that have information in them. NOTE - do not select any blank cells!
2. Pull down the **Options** menu to **Make Chart**.
3. Choose the Bar option.
4. Click the Label button.
5. Enter the title, "Eye Color."
6. Click the General button.
7. Change the Series to Rows.
8. Click OK; SAVE!

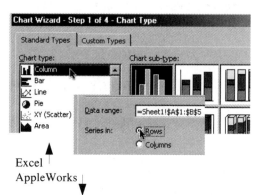

Excel
AppleWorks

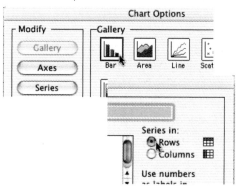

Changing bar colors:
Excel:
1. Double click a bar on the chart.
2. Click the Patterns tab.
3. Click to choose a color.

AppleWorks:
1. Click the square beside one of the colors in the legend.
2. Choose a color using the color palette in the tools menu. Note - if the tools aren't showing, pull down the **Window** menu to **Show Tools**.

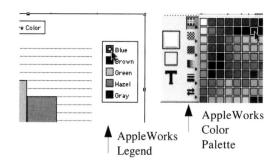

AppleWorks
Legend

AppleWorks
Color
Palette

Extensions:
• Students can work in pairs or teams to complete the activity.
• Students can chart different class data; height, shoe size, hair color, arm span, hand size, etc.

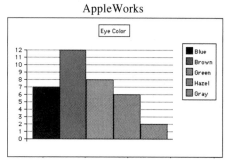

AppleWorks

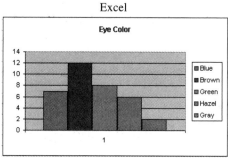

Excel

Magic Square

Grade Level:
- K
- 1
- 2
- • 3
- • 4
- • 5
- • 6

Content Area:
- • Math
- Language Arts
- Social Studies
- Science
- • Cross Curricular

Multiple Intelligences:
- Verbal / Linguistic
- • Logical / Mathematical
- Spatial
- Bodily / Kinesthetic
- Musical
- Interpersonal
- Intrapersonal
- Naturalist

CD-ROM Templates:
- 22magicsquare.xls - Microsoft Excel
- 22magicsquare.cwk - AppleWorks

Overview:
In this activity, students will create and then solve a math puzzle using a spreadsheet.

Software:
Microsoft Excel or AppleWorks Spreadsheet

ISTE Standards:
- Students use technology tools to process data and report results.
- Students use technology resources for solving problems and making informed decisions.

The Teacher's Role:
1. The teacher will introduce the students to the spreadsheet. (See information below.)
2. The teacher will demonstrate how to change the sizes and add borders to cells.
3. The teacher will show students how to add formulas.
4. The teacher will challenge the students to complete the puzzle.

Introduction to the spreadsheet:

The spreadsheet is a document made up of COLUMNS and ROWS. Columns are labeled with letters (a, b, c, etc.) and rows are labeled with numbers (1, 2, 3, etc.) Where a column and row intersect, a rectangle is created. The rectangle is called a CELL.

Each cell has its own ADDRESS. The address is a combination of the Column letter and the row number. The cell in the upper left corner is cell A1. (Just like playing Battleship!) *Call out various cell addresses and have the students click them.*

FORMULAS can be entered into cells to calculate data (add numbers, multiply numbers, etc.).

Student Instructions:

Setting up the Magic Square:
1. Open a Microsoft Excel or AppleWorks Spreadsheet document.
2. Click and drag from cell A1 to D4 to highlight the cells.
3. Resize the cells:

In Excel:
> a. Pull down the **Format** menu to **Row** and over to **Height**.
> b. Set the Row Height to 50.
> c. Pull down the **Format** menu to **Column** and over to **Width**.
> d. Set the Column Width to 8.

In AppleWorks
> a. Pull down the **Format** menu to **Row Height**.
> b. Set the Row Height at 60.
> c. Pull down the **Format** menu to **Column Width**.
> d. Set the Column Width to 60.

4. While A1 to D4 are highlighted, add borders:

In Excel:
> a. Pull down the **Format** menu to **Cells**.
> b. Click the Border tab.
> c. Click the Outline button and the Inside button.

In AppleWorks
> a. Pull down the **Insert** menu to **Borders**.
> b. Click to check all border options.

5. While A1 to D4 are highlighted, change the font size to 24.

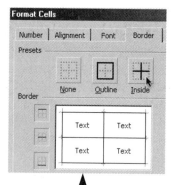

Excel Borders
AppleWorks Borders

Adding formulas:
1. Click each cell and enter each formula as shown at the right.
2. Be SURE to begin each formula with the equal sign.
3. Be SURE to press the Return or Enter key on your keyboard after entering each formula.
4. SAVE!

Solving the puzzle:
> Enter the numbers 0-9 in the blank 9 squares (A1 through C3) so that each outside square equals 15. You can only enter each number ONE time!

Student challenge:
See if you can add colors to the cells of the magic square.

In cell:	Enter formula:
D1	=A1+B1+C1
D2	=A2+B2+C2
D3	=A3+B3+C3
D4	=A1+B2+C3
A4	=A1+A2+A3
B4	=B1+B2+B3
C4	=C1+C2+C3

Extensions:
• Students could work in pairs or teams to complete the activity.
• Students could add clip art to their magic square.

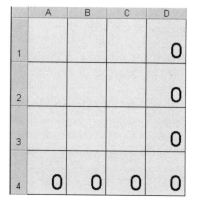

Pizza Pie Graph

Grade Level:
K
1
• 2
• 3
• 4
• 5
• 6

Content Area:
• Math
  Language Arts
• Social Studies
  Science
• Cross Curricular

Multiple Intelligences:
  Verbal / Linguistic
• Logical / Mathematical
• Spatial
  Bodily / Kinesthetic
  Musical
• Interpersonal
  Intrapersonal
  Naturalist

CD-ROM Templates:
• 23pizzagraph.xls - Microsoft Excel
• 23pizzagraph.cwk - AppleWorks

Overview:
In this activity, students will use a spreadsheet to create a pie graph that shows the class's favorite types of pizza.

Software:
Microsoft Excel or AppleWorks Spreadsheet

ISTE Standards:
• Students use technology to locate, evaluate, and collect information from a variety of sources.
• Students use technology tools to process data and report results.

The Teacher's Role:
1. The teacher will conduct a poll to find out the students' favorite types of pizza. (Just name a type of pizza and have students raise their hands.)
2. The teacher will record the results and will post them where all students can see them. (example:. Pepperoni - 10; Cheese - 7; Sausage - 3; Beef - 4; Combination - 1)
3. The teacher will demonstrate how to enter the data into a spreadsheet.
4. The teacher will show the students how to turn their data into a pie graph.

Note -- If the students are not familiar with the spreadsheet, you may want to refer to the information at the bottom of page 43.

Student Instructions:

Entering the Data:

1. Open a new Microsoft Excel or AppleWorks Spreadsheet document.
2. Enter the types of pizza in column A.
3. Enter the numbers in column B.

Creating the Chart:

Excel:

1. Click and drag to select all cells that have information in them. NOTE - do not select any blank cells!
2. Pull down the **Insert** menu to **Chart**.
3. Choose the Pie option.
4. Click the Next button twice to get to Step 3.
5. Enter the title, "Favorite Pizza".
6. Click Finish; SAVE!

Appleworks:

1. Click and drag to select all cells that have information in them. NOTE - do not select any blank cells!
2. Pull down the **Options** menu to **Make Chart**.
3. Choose the Pie option.
4. Click the Label button.
5. Enter the title, "Favorite Pizza".
6. Click OK; SAVE!

Student Challenges:

(Use the help menu if necessary.)

• Can you change the colors of the pie "pieces"?
• Can you add labels so that each pie piece shows a number or percentage?
• Can you change the color of the background of the chart?

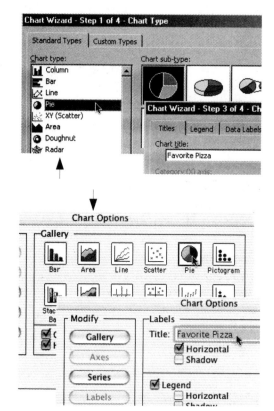

Extensions:

• Students can work in pairs or teams to complete the activity.
• Students can chart different class favorites: soft drinks; TV shows; sports teams; actors; musicians; colors; etc.

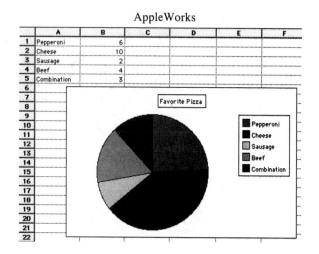

AppleWorks

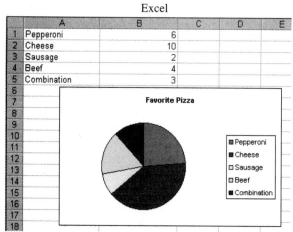

Excel

Planet Weigh-In

Grade Level:
K
1
2
• 3
• 4
• 5
• 6

Content Area:
• Math
  Language Arts
  Social Studies
• Science
• Cross Curricular

Multiple Intelligences:
  Verbal / Linguistic
• Logical / Mathematical
  Spatial
  Bodily / Kinesthetic
  Musical
  Interpersonal
  Intrapersonal
• Naturalist

CD-ROM Templates:
• 24planet.xls - Microsoft Excel
• 24planet.cwk - AppleWorks

Overview:
In this activity, students will use a spreadsheet to design a planet weight calculator. When the students enter the weight of an object on Earth, it will automatically calculate its weight on the other planets.

Software:
Microsoft Excel or AppleWorks Spreadsheet

ISTE Standards:
• Students use technology tools to process data and report results.
• Students use technology resources for solving problems and making informed decisions.

The Teacher's Role:
1. The teacher will introduce students to the spreadsheet.
   Note - if students are unfamiliar with the spreadsheet, use the introduction at the bottom of page 43.
2. The teacher will show students how to add borders to cells of the spreadsheet.
3. The teacher will provide the formulas and will show the students how to enter them.

Student Instructions:

Setting up the Planet Weight Calculator:
1. Open a Microsoft Excel or AppleWorks Spreadsheet document.
2. Click and drag from cell A1 to D4 to highlight the cells.
3. In cell A1, enter "Weight on Earth:".
4. In cell A4, enter "Weight on:".
5. In cells A5 through A12, enter the planets in this order:
   Mercury, Venus, Mars, Jupiter, Saturn, Uranus, Neptune, Pluto.

Adding borders to cells:
Excel:
1. Click into Cell B2.
   a. Pull down the **Format** menu to **Cells**.
   b. Click the Border tab.
   c. Click the Outline button.
2. Click and drag to highlight cells B5 through B12.
   a. Pull down the **Format** menu to **Cells**.
   b. Click the Border tab.
   c. Click the Outline button; then click the Inside button.

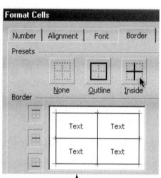

Excel Borders
AppleWorks Borders

AppleWorks
1. Click into Cell B2.
   a. Pull down the **Format** menu to **Borders**.
   b. Click to check the Outline button.
2. Click and drag to highlight cells B5 through B12.
   a. Pull down the **Insert** menu to **Borders**.
   b. Click to check all options.

Adding formulas:
1. Click each cell and enter each formula as shown at the right.
2. Be SURE to begin each formula with the equal sign.
3. Be SURE to press the Return or Enter key on your keyboard after entering each formula.

In Cell:	Enter Formula:
B5	=B2*.378
B6	=B2*.907
B7	=B2*.377
B8	=B2*2.364
B9	=B2*.916
B10	=B2*.889
B11	=B2*1.125
B12	=B2*.067

Formatting the Numbers:
1. Click and drag to select cells B5 through B12.
   Appleworks - Pull down the **Format** menu to **Number**. Choose the Fixed option.
   Excel - Pull down the **Format** menu to **Cells**. Click the Number tab and choose the Number option.
2. SAVE!

Using the calculator
1. Enter a weight of an object on earth in cell B2.
2. Look at the other cells to see how much the object would weigh on each of the other planets.

	A	B
1	Weight on Earth:	
2		50
3		
4	Weight on:	
5	Mercury	18.90
6	Venus	45.35
7	Mars	18.85
8	Jupiter	118.20
9	Saturn	45.80
10	Uranus	44.45
11	Neptune	56.25
12	Pluto	3.35
13		

Extensions:
• Students can work in pairs or teams to complete the activity.
• Students can add colors and clip art to the spreadsheet.

The Power of a Penny

Grade Level:
K
1
2
• 3
• 4
• 5
• 6

Content Area:
• Math
Language Arts
• Social Studies
Science
• Cross Curricular

Multiple Intelligences:
• Verbal / Linguistic
• Logical / Mathematical
Spatial
Bodily / Kinesthetic
Musical
Interpersonal
Intrapersonal
Naturalist

CD-ROM Templates:
• 25penny.xls - Microsoft Excel
• 25penny.cwk - AppleWorks

Overview:
Students will be given this scenario: "Would you rather take $1,000,000 right now, or take a penny that doubles every day for a month?" Students will then use a spreadsheet to calculate the results.

Software:
Microsoft Excel or AppleWorks Spreadsheet

ISTE Standards:
• Students use technology tools to process data and report results.
• Students use technology resources for solving problems and making informed decisions.

The Teacher's Role:
1. The teacher will give the students this scenario: "Would you rather take $1,000,000 right now, or a penny that doubles every day for a month?"
2. The teacher will show the students how to enter the information and formulas into the spreadsheet.
3. The teacher will show the students how to add a formula to total the amount.

Student Instructions:

Getting Ready

1. Open a Microsoft Excel or AppleWorks Spreadsheet document.
2. In cell A1, enter "Day."
3. In cell B1, enter "Amount."
4. In cells A2 through A32, enter the numbers 1 through 31.
5. In cell B2, enter .01. (The value of a penny)
6. In cell A34, enter "Total:".
7. Resize column B to make it about twice as wide as column A.
   a. Move your mouse into the header area where the letters A, B, and C are.
   b. Move your mouse onto the line directly between the B and C.
   c. Click and drag to the right to make column B larger.

Formatting the cells

Appleworks

1. Click and drag to select cells B2 through B34.
2. Pull down the **Format** menu to **Number**.
3. Choose the Currency option.
4. Click to Show Separators for Thousands.

Excel

1. Click and drag to select cells B2 through B34.
2. Pull down the **Format** menu to **Cells**.
3. Click the Number tab.
4. Choose the Currency option.

Entering the formulas

1. Click into cell B3.
2. Enter the formula: =B2*2
3. Click into cell B34.
4. Enter the formula: =Sum(B2:B32)

Filling down the formula

Appleworks

1. Click and drag from cell B2 through B32.
2. Pull down the **Calculate** menu to **Fill Down**.
3. SAVE!

Excel

1. Click into cell B3.
2. Look for the small square in the lower right corner of the cell.
3. Click and drag the small square down to cell B32.
4. SAVE!

Coming to a conclusion

1. Look at the total in cell B34.
2. Are you surprised by the result?

Extensions:

• Students can work in pairs or groups to complete the activity.
• The teacher could invite a banker or investment counselor to talk to the students about the power of compound interest.

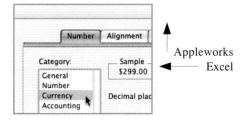

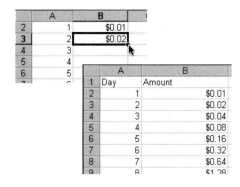

Wish List Calculator

Grade Level:
K
1
2
• 3
• 4
• 5
• 6

Content Area:
• Math
  Language Arts
• Social Studies
  Science
• Cross Curricular

Multiple Intelligences:
Verbal / Linguistic
• Logical / Mathematical
Spatial
Bodily / Kinesthetic
Musical
• Interpersonal
• Intrapersonal
Naturalist

CD-ROM Templates:
• 26wishlist.xls - Microsoft Excel
• 26wishlist.cwk - AppleWorks

Overview:
In this activity, students will set up a spreadsheet that will calculate the subtotals and the total of their wish lists.

Software:
Microsoft Excel or AppleWorks.

ISTE Standards:
• Students use technology tools to process data and report results.
• Students use technology resources for solving problems and making informed decisions.

Web Resources:
Toys-R-Us - www.toysrus.com
eToys - www.etoys.com

The Teacher's Role:
1. The teacher will introduce the students to the spreadsheet. (Refer to the Magic Square directions.)
2. The teacher will demonstrate how to change the sizes of columns and rows.
3. The teacher will show students how to add formulas.
4. The teacher will demonstrate how to add items to the wish list.

Note - The teacher may want to provide catalogs or sales fliers that include toys and prices.

Student Instructions:

Setting up the spreadsheet:
1. Open a Microsoft Excel or AppleWorks Spreadsheet document.
2. Resize the columns and rows to look like the image at the right:

   To resize a column:
   a. Move your mouse into the header area where the letters A, B, and C are.
   b. Move your mouse onto the line directly between two columns.
   c. To make the column wider, click and drag to the right; to make the column narrower, click and drag to the left.

   To resize a row:
   a. Move your mouse into the header area where the numbers 1, 2, and 3 are.
   b. Move your mouse onto the line directly between two rows.
   c. To make the row longer, click and drag down; to make the row shorter, click and drag up.

   Note - Rows 2 and 13 are narrow to create dividers.

Adding Labels:
1. Add the following labels in row 1:
   Qty | Item | Price Each | Subtotal
2. In cell D14, enter the word "Total".

Formatting the Numbers:
1. Click and drag to select cells C3 through D14.
   Appleworks - Pull down the **Format** menu to **Number**. Choose the Currency option.
   Excel - Pull down the **Format** menu to **Cells**. Click the Number tab and choose the Currency option.

Adding the formulas:
1. Click each cell and enter each formula as shown at the right.
2. Be SURE to begin each formula with the equal sign.
3. Be SURE to press the Return or Enter key on your keyboard after entering each formula.

Student Challenge:
   Use the Help menu to find out how to "fill down" the formula you entered in cell D3.

Entering the Wish List:
1. Enter up to 10 items and prices from your wish list.
2. The spreadsheet should automatically calculate the subtotals and totals.
3. SAVE!

Extensions:
• Students could be given a spending limit.
• Instead of a *wish* list, students could create a *gift* list of things they want to give others.
• Students could add colors to the cells of their wish list.
• Students could change fonts, sizes, styles, and colors.
• Students could add pictures and/or clip art.

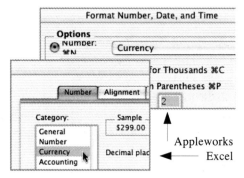

In Cell:	Enter the formula:
D3	=A3*C3
D4	=A4*C4
D5	=A5*C5
D6	=A6*C6
D7	=A7*C7
D8	=A8*C8
D9	=A9*C9
D10	=A10*C10
D11	=A11*C11
D12	=A12*C12
D14	=SUM(DE:D13)

	A	B	C	D
1	Qty	Item	Price Each	Subtotal
3	1	Bicycle	$299.00	$299.00
4	1	XBOX	$200.00	$200.00
5	3	Games for XBOX	$50.00	$150.00
6				
7				
8				
9				
10				
11				
12				
14			TOTAL	$649.00

Brainstorming!

Grade Level:
K
1
2
• 3
• 4
• 5
• 6

Content Area:
• Math
• Language Arts
• Social Studies
  Science
• Cross Curricular

Multiple Intelligences:
• Verbal / Linguistic
• Logical / Mathematical
  Spatial
  Bodily / Kinesthetic
  Musical
  Interpersonal
  Intrapersonal
  Naturalist

CD-ROM Templates:
• 27brainstorming - Inspiration

Overview:
In this activity, students will brainstorm as many ideas as they can using the Inspiration program.

Software:
Inspiration

ISTE Standards:
• Students develop positive attitudes toward technology uses that support lifelong learning, collaboration, personal pursuits, and productivity.
• Students use technology tools to enhance learning, increase productivity, and promote creativity.

The Teacher's Role:
1. The teacher will give the students a topic to brainstorm.
2. The teacher will show the students how to use the rapid fire option to quickly add "bubbles" to the diagram.
   NOTE - this activity can be done using the Kidspiration program, but no "rapid fire" option will be available.

Brainstorm Topic Ideas:
• uses for a paper clip
• things that are blue, green, pink, etc.
• things that have four legs
• ways to make someone laugh
• things with 3 sides or things with 4 sides
• homophones
• ways to say hello, goodbye, yes, no, etc.
• ways to get to Hawaii
• reasons to eat healthy foods

Student Instructions:

1. Open a new Inspiration document.
2. For the main idea or first idea, enter the brainstorm topic.
3. Click the Rapid Fire icon at the top of the screen.
4. Enter your first idea.
5. Press the Return or Enter key on your keyboard.
6. Continue entering ideas, pressing the Return or Enter key after each idea.

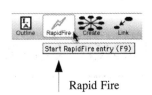

Rapid Fire

Fancying your diagram:

1. Change the colors of your symbols, using the color tools at the bottom of the screen.
2. Change the shapes of your symbols, using the symbol palette at the left.
3. Add clip art from the symbol palette by dragging the clips onto the screen.
4. SAVE!

Extensions:

• Students could work in pairs or teams to complete the activity.
• Prizes could be awarded to the student, pair, or team that generates the most ideas.
• Students could come up with their own brainstorm topics.

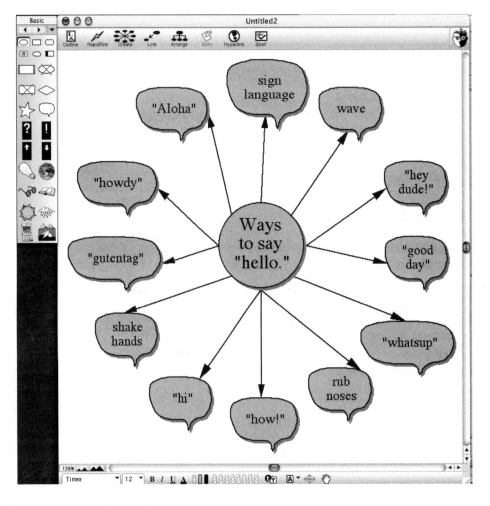

Color Quatrain

Grade Level:
- K
- 1
- • 2
- • 3
- • 4
- • 5
- • 6

Content Area:
- Math
- • Language Arts
- Social Studies
- Science
- • Cross Curricular

Multiple Intelligences:
- • Verbal / Linguistic
- Logical / Mathematical
- Spatial
- Bodily / Kinesthetic
- Musical
- Interpersonal
- Intrapersonal
- • Naturalist

CD-ROM Templates:
- 28quantrain.kid - Kidspiration

Overview:
In this activity, students write a quatrain about colors and then publish it using Inspiration or Kidspiration.

Software:
Inspiration or Kidspiration

ISTE Standards:
- Students develop positive attitudes toward technology uses that support lifelong learning, collaboration, personal pursuits, and productivity.
- Students use technology tools to enhance learning, increase productivity, and promote creativity.

Web Resources:
Poetry4Kids - http://www.poetry4kids.com/
GigglePoetry - http://www.gigglepoetry.com/
Fizzy Funny Fuzzy - http://www.fizzyfunnyfuzzy.com/
Word Central (Music Room) Rhyming Dictionary - www.wordcentral.com

The Teacher's Role:
1. The teacher will introduce the students to the quatrain (any 4-lined poem).
2. The teacher will read examples of quatrains.
3. The teacher will instruct the students to write a quatrain about colors.
4. The teacher will show the students how to enter their poems into an Inspiration or Kidspiration document.

Student Instructions:

Getting Started

1. Write your own 4-line poem about colors. Note - you may want lines 1 and 2 to rhyme and lines 3 and 4 to rhyme. OR you could rhyme 1 and 3, and 2 and 4!
2. Open a new Inspiration or Kidspiration document.
3. Enter the first line of your poem.
4. Click below the first "bubble" and begin typing to enter the second line of your poem.
5. Add lines three and four of your poem.

Fancying your Document

1. Click the top "bubble" to select it.
2. To change the shape, choose one of the top icons from the symbol palette.
3. To change the color, choose a color from the pop-up color palette at the bottom of the screen.
4. Repeat steps 1-3 to change the shapes and colors of each line of your poem.
5. Click the arrows at the top of the symbol palette to view the clip art.
6. Click and drag clip art from the symbol palette onto the screen.
7. SAVE!
8. Print your poem and glue it onto a larger sheet of colored paper.

Change shapes

Change Colors

Extensions:

• Students could write quatrains that include facts for any content area.
• Students could write poems for different holidays.
• Students could write poems about themselves.
• Students could work in pairs or teams to create quatrains.

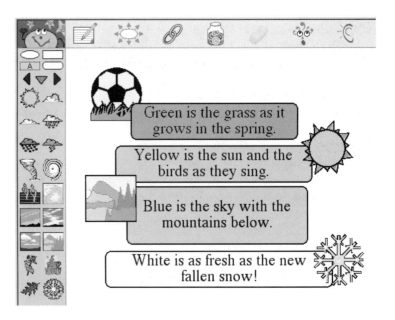

29

Debating an Issue

Grade Level:
K
1
2
• 3
• 4
• 5
• 6

Content Area:
Math
• Language Arts
• Social Studies
Science
• Cross Curricular

Multiple Intelligences:
• Verbal / Linguistic
• Logical / Mathematical
Spatial
Bodily / Kinesthetic
Musical
• Interpersonal
Intrapersonal
Naturalist

CD-ROM Templates:
• 29debate.kid - Kidspiration

Overview:
In this activity, students will brainstorm options / reasons for both sides of an issue using the Kidspiration or Inspiration program.

Software:
Inspiration or Kidspiration

ISTE Standards:
• Students develop positive attitudes toward technology uses that support lifelong learning, collaboration, personal pursuits, and productivity.
• Students use technology tools to enhance learning, increase productivity, and promote creativity.

The Teacher's Role:
1. The teacher will give the students a debate topic or issue.
2. The teacher will show the students how to add "bubbles" to an Inspiration or Kidspiration document.
3. The teacher will demonstrate how to add clip art to the document.

Debate Issue Ideas:
• There should be no speed limits.
• Gum chewing should be allowed in class.
• Kids should choose their own bed time.
• We should have longer recesses.
• The cafeteria should serve only junk food.
• Kids should be able to vote.
• Our school should / shouldn't have a dress code.
• Teachers shouldn't be allowed to give tests.

Student Instructions:
1. Open a new Inspiration or Kidspiration document.
2. For the main idea or first idea, enter the debate issue sentence. (ex. There should be no speed limits.)
3. Click the "Create" or "Add symbol" tool to add two symbols that are linked to your first bubble.
4. Add the words "Why?" and "Why Not" to the two new symbols.
5. Brainstorm ideas and reasons to support both sides of the issue.
6. Add each idea as a new linked symbol.

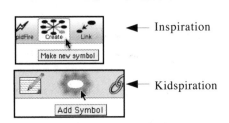

← Inspiration

← Kidspiration

Fancying your diagram:
1. Change the colors of your symbols using the color tools at the bottom of the screen.
2. Change the shapes of your symbols using the symbol palette at the left.
3. Add clip art from the symbol palette by dragging the clips onto the screen.
4. SAVE!

Extensions:
• Students could work in pairs or teams to complete the activity.
• Students could brainstorm their own debate topics.
• The teacher could divide the class into two teams and have a verbal debate over the issue.

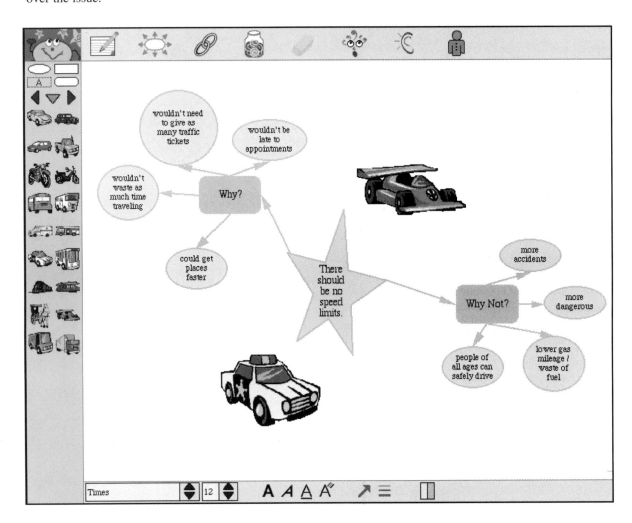

Map-It

Grade Level:
- K
- 1
- 2
- 3
- 4
- 5
- 6

Content Area:
Math
Language Arts
- Social Studies
Science
- Cross Curricular

Multiple Intelligences:
Verbal / Linguistic
- Logical / Mathematical
- Spatial
Bodily / Kinesthetic
Musical
Interpersonal
Intrapersonal
Naturalist

CD-ROM Templates:
• 30map.kid - Kidspiration

Overview:
In this activity, students will use a map-generator Web site to create a map of their city / town / community. Then they add clip art to label different areas such as their house, their school, the hospital, etc.

Software:
Inspiration or Kidspiration
Other Paint / Draw programs

ISTE Standards:
• Students develop positive attitudes toward technology uses that support lifelong learning, collaboration, personal pursuits, and productivity.
• Students use technology tools to enhance learning, increase productivity, and promote creativity.

Web Resources:
MapQuest - www.mapquest.com
Yahoo Maps - http://maps.yahoo.com

The Teacher's Role:
1. The teacher will show the students how to generate a map using an online map program.
2. The teacher will demonstrate how to copy the map and paste it into an Inspiration or Kidspiration document.
3. The teacher will show students how to add icons to their map.

Student Instructions:
Creating / Copying the Map
1. Open the MapQuest (or Yahoo Maps) Web site.
2. Enter the name of your city and state.
3. Click the "Get Map" or "Create Map" button.
4. Click the zoom buttons until you see a map that shows just your community.
5. Click the "Print Map" link at the top of the map. (This will create a larger view of your map.)
6. Move your mouse to the center of the map.
7. To copy the map:
   Macintosh - Click and hold the mouse button.
   Windows - Click the right mouse button.
   From the menu, choose "Copy" or "Copy Image".

In Inspiration / Kidspiration
1. Open a new Inspiration or Kidspiration document.
2. Pull down the **Edit** menu to **Paste**. (Your map should appear on the screen.)
3. Click away from the map to deselect it.
4. Use the arrows at the top of the symbol palette to browse the clip art. (Look for images to represent things in your community: school, hospital, grocery story, church, etc.)
5. Drag the clip art images onto the map. Make sure you put them in the right places!
6. SAVE!

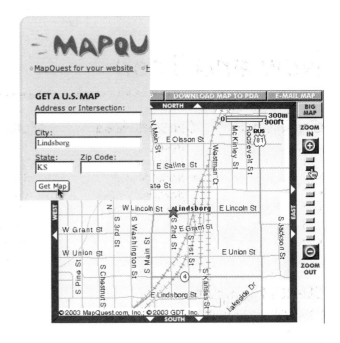

Extensions:
- Older students could write step by step instruction for getting from one place on the map to another.
- Students could add the actual address of each place on the map.
- Students could add a legend to show what each icon represents.

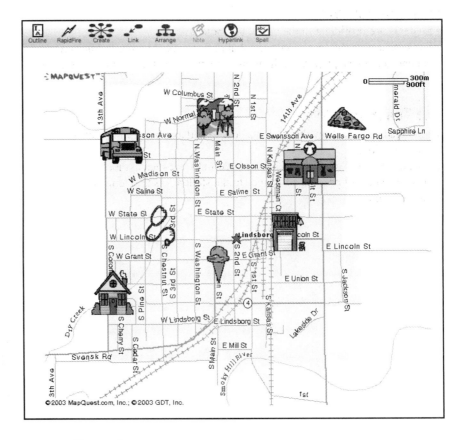

Now and Then

Grade Level:
- K
- 1
- • 2
- • 3
- • 4
- • 5
- • 6

Content Area:
- Math
- • Language Arts
- • Social Studies
- Science
- • Cross Curricular

Multiple Intelligences:
- • Verbal / Linguistic
- Logical / Mathematical
- Spatial
- Bodily / Kinesthetic
- Musical
- Interpersonal
- • Intrapersonal
- Naturalist

CD-ROM Templates:
- 31nowthen.isf - Inspiration

Overview:
In this activity, students will use the Inspiration or Kidspiration program to compare what they do now with what they think they'll be doing when they are 30 years old.

Software:
Inspiration or Kidspiration

ISTE Standards:
- Students are proficient in the use of technology.
- Students use productivity tools to collaborate in constructing technology-enhanced models, prepare publications, and produce other creative works.

The Teacher's Role:
1. The teacher will show the students how to add symbols in Inspiration or Kidspiration.
2. The teacher will demonstrate how to add links between symbols.
3. The teacher will provide assistance to the students as they think about their future.

Student Instructions:

1. Open a new Inspiration or Kidspiration document.
2. Enter your name as the first idea or main idea.
3. Click and drag your name to the top of the screen.
4. Click the Create or Add Symbol button to add two linked "bubbles."
5. In the left bubble, enter "Now (your age)." In the right bubble, enter "When I'm 30".
6. Add symbols and links as shown below to compare:
   •What I do •Where I live •My Income •My Family •Transportation
7. Change the shapes of symbols using the symbol palette.
8. Change colors and fonts, using the tool bar at the bottom of the screen.
9. Add clip art if you want.
10. SAVE!

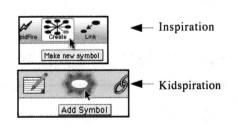

◄—— Inspiration

◄—— Kidspiration

Working with links:

To add a link between symbols:
1. Click the "Link" button in the tool bar at the top of the screen.
2. Click the bubble you want to link *from*.
3. Click the bubble you want to link *to*.

To remove a link:
1. Click the center of the link line to select it.
2. Press the Delete key on your keyboard.

Extensions:

• Students could add additional items to compare: How I look, My house, My Hobbies, etc.
• Students could add predictions for "When I'm 70".

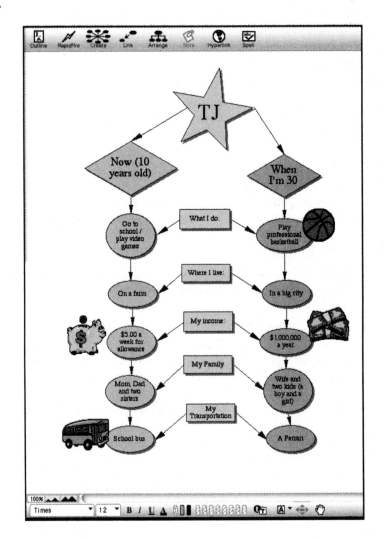

Pleaase do not copy.

Number Autobiography

Grade Level:
- K (with help)
- 1 (with help)
- 2
- 3
- 4
- 5
- 6

Content Area:
Math
- Language Arts
- Social Studies
Science
- Cross Curricular

Multiple Intelligences:
- Verbal / Linguistic
- Logical / Mathematical
Spatial
Bodily / Kinesthetic
Musical
Interpersonal
- Intrapersonal
Naturalist

CD-ROM Templates:
• 32autobiography.isf - Inspiration

Overview:
In this activity, students will write about something interesting that happened to them for each year of their life. They will organize it into a top down tree or a right tree in the Inspiration program.

Software:
Inspiration or Kidspiration*

* If the Kidspiration program is used, students will need to physically arrange their diagram by clicking and dragging the symbols. (There is no arrange tool in Kidspiration.)

ISTE Standards:
• Students are proficient in the use of technology.
• Students use technology tools to process data and report results.

Web Resources:
Inspiration - www.inspiration.com (Download a 30-day trial version.)
Kidspiration - www.kidspiration.com (Download a 30-day trial version.)

The Teacher's Role:
1. The teacher will describe the activity to the students.
2. The teacher will instruct the students to think about something exciting or interesting that has happened in each year of their life. (They may want to ask their parents for help.)
3. The teacher will make sure the students have a rough draft of their number autobiography before they go to the computer.
4. The teacher will show the students how to enter and arrange their information using Inspiration.
5. The teacher will demonstrate how to add clip art.
6. The teacher will show the students how to print their number autobiographies.

Student Instructions:

Preparing the rough draft

1. Write the numbers 0, 1, 2, etc. down the left side of a sheet of paper. (If you are 8 years old, write the numbers 0-8; if you are 10, write the numbers 0-10, etc.)

2. Beside each number, write something interesting that happened to you when you were that age. You may want to get some help from your parents, grandparents, or other adults.

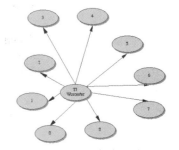

At the computer:

1. Open the Inspiration program.
2. Replace "new idea" with your name.
3. Create new symbols and enter each number.
3. Create a new symbol from each number symbol and enter your interesting fact.
4. Click the Arrange button in the tool bar at the top of the screen and try different arrangements until you find one you like.

   NOTE - after arranging, press these keys on your keyboard to center your diagram and fit it to the screen:

   Macintosh - Apple and E
   Windows - Control and E

Fancying your diagram:

1. Change the colors of your symbols using the color tools at the bottom of the screen.
2. Change the shapes of your symbols, using the symbol palette at the left.
3. Add clip art from the symbol palette by dragging the clips onto the screen.
4. SAVE!

Extensions:

• Students could add a digital picture of themselves!

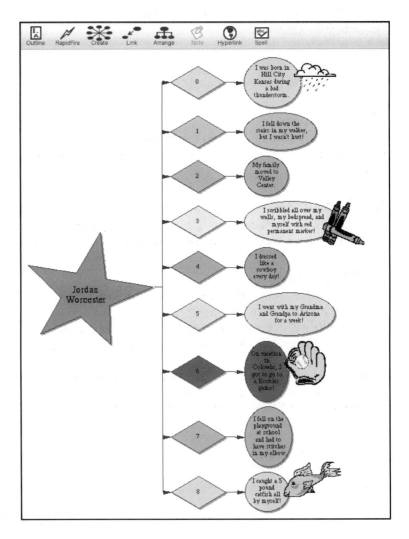

Pleaase do not copy.

Story Map Mobile

Grade Level:	**Content Area:**	**Multiple Intelligences:**
K	Math	• Verbal / Linguistic
1	• Language Arts	Logical / Mathematical
• 2	Social Studies	• Spatial
• 3	Science	• Bodily / Kinesthetic
• 4	• Cross Curricular	Musical
• 5		• Interpersonal
• 6		Intrapersonal
		Naturalist

CD-ROM Templates:
• 33storymap.kid - Kidspiration

Overview:
In this activity, students will create a story map using Inspiration or Kidspiration shapes. Then they will print, cut around the shapes and hang them from string or thread to create a mobile.

Software:
Inspiration or Kidspiration

ISTE Standards:
• Students are proficient in the use of technology.
• Students use technology tools to enhance learning, increase productivity, and promote creativity.

Web Resources:
Inspiration - www.inspiration.com (Download a 30-day trial version.)
Kidspiration - www.kidspiration.com (Download a 30-day trial version.)

The Teacher's Role:
1. The teacher will instruct the students to think about a character from a story they've read or heard.
2. The teacher will direct them to complete a story map with the following format: A character __ ; wanted to __ ; but __ ; so __ .
3. The teacher will show the students how to create symbols for the title and map. (see student instructions).
4. The teacher will direct the students to print, cut, and assemble their mobile.

Student Instructions:
Creating the character map:
1. Choose a character from a story you've read or heard.
2. Complete the following:
   A character _____.
   wanted to _____.
   but _____.
   so _____.
3. Open an Inspiration or Kidspiration document.
4. Create symbols as shown in the picture at the right.
5. Print 2 copies.
6. Cut around each of the shapes. (You will have two of each.)

Assembling the mobile:
1. Cut 4 pieces of string (or thread) 6-8 inches long.
2. Apply glue to the back of one "title" shape.
3. Place the ends of the 4 pieces of string on the "title" shape as shown at the right.
4. Loop the 5th piece of string at the top. (You can use this to hang the mobile.)
5. Place the second "title" shape on top so that the titles are showing on both sides.
6. Place glue on the backs of the oval shapes and "sandwich" the center of the threads.
7. Place glue on the backs of the rounded rectangle shapes and "sandwich" the bottom of the threads.
8. SAVE!

Extensions:
• Students could create a mobile to report an event. Categories could include:
  - who?
  - what?
  - when?
  - where?
  - why?

• Students could create a book review mobile with categories:
  - author
  - main character(s)
  - plot
  - setting
  - recommendation

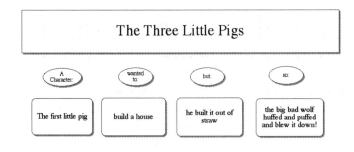

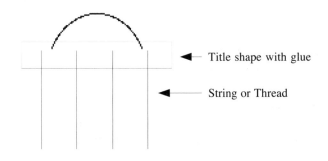

Title shape with glue

String or Thread

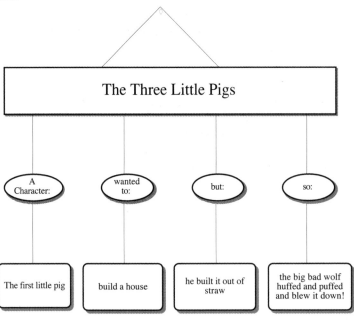

Wouldn't It Be Cool If...

Grade Level:
K
1
2
• 3
• 4
• 5
• 6

Content Area:
Math
• Language Arts
Social Studies
Science
• Cross Curricular

Multiple Intelligences:
• Verbal / Linguistic
• Logical / Mathematical
Spatial
Bodily / Kinesthetic
Musical
Interpersonal
Intrapersonal
Naturalist

CD-ROM Templates:
• 34cool.isf - Inspiration

Overview:
In this project, students will choose clip art items and will complete the sentence, "Wouldn't It Be Cool If..." for each clip.

Software:
Inspiration or Kidspiration
Other Painting / Drawing Program

ISTE Standards:
• Students develop positive attitudes toward technology uses that support lifelong learning, collaboration, personal pursuits, and productivity.
• Students use technology tools to enhance learning, increase productivity, and promote creativity.

The Teacher's Role:
1. The teacher can introduce the activity by leading a "what if?" discussion. Ask the question, "What if you could create your own school?", and have students share their answers.
2. The teacher will demonstrate how to add images and text to an Inspiration / Kidspiration screen.

Student Instructions:

1. Open a new Inspiration or Kidspiration document.
2. For the main idea or first idea, enter the text "Wouldn't it be cool if...".
3. Use the arrows at the top of the symbol palette to look through the clip art.
4. Choose an image.
5. Click and drag the image onto the screen.
6. Click below the image to complete the "Wouldn't it be cool if..." sentence.
7. Use the text tools at the bottom of the screen to change fonts, sizes, colors, etc.
8. Click and drag to move the title and images where you want them to be.
9. SAVE and print!

Kidspiration

Inspiration

Extensions:

• Students could do the opposite and finish the sentence, "Aren't you glad that..."
• Students can work in pairs or teams to complete the activity.

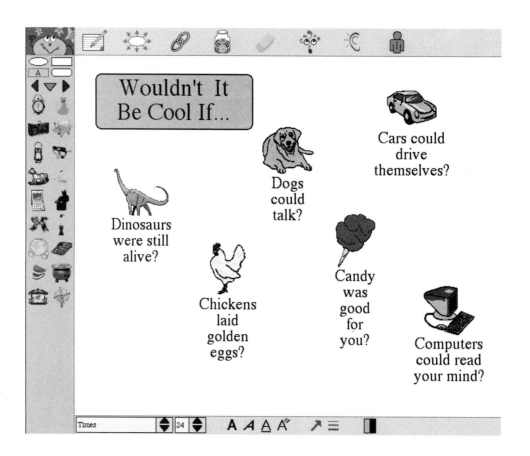

Choose Your Own Ending

Grade Level:
K
1
2
• 3
• 4
• 5
• 6

Content Area:
Math
• Language Arts
Social Studies
Science
• Cross Curricular

Multiple Intelligences:
• Verbal / Linguistic
• Logical / Mathematical
Spatial
Bodily / Kinesthetic
Musical
Interpersonal
Intrapersonal
Naturalist

CD-ROM Templates:
• 35chooseending - Microsoft PowerPoint

Overview:
In this activity, students will write a story with 3 optional endings. They will put their story into an interactive slide show. Readers will be able to click a button to choose an ending for the story.

Software:
Microsoft PowerPoint

ISTE Standards:
• Students develop positive attitudes toward technology uses that support lifelong learning, collaboration, personal pursuits, and productivity.
• Students use a variety of media and formats to communicate information and ideas effectively to multiple audiences.

The Teacher's Role:
1. The teacher will instruct the students to write a short story with three different endings.
2. The teacher will show the students how to enter their story into PowerPoint slides.
3. The teacher will demonstrate how to add buttons that will take the viewer to different endings.

Student Instructions:

Writing the Story:
1. Write a short story.
2. Write 3 different endings for the story.

Creating the Title Slide:
1. Open a new PowerPoint document.
2. Choose the Title Slide layout option.
3. Enter your story's title and your name.
4. Change the font size if you want.

Creating the slides
1. Pull down the **Insert** menu to **New Slide**.
2. Choose the Blank slide layout option.
3. Use the text tool to type part of your story.
4. Use the drawing tools or clip art to add a picture if you want.
5. Repeat steps 1-4 until you have entered your story with a slide for each ending.

Creating the buttons
1. Move to the "choose an ending" slide.
2. Click the AutoShapes tool and pull up to Action Buttons; Pull over to choose a button.
3. Click and drag to add a button to your screen.
4. In the Action Settings menu, choose to Hyperlink to: SLIDE.
5. Choose the slide you want to link to.
6. Repeat steps 1-5 to create two more buttons on this slide.
7. SAVE!

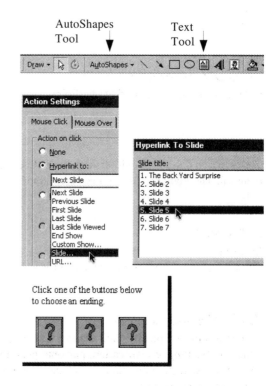

Student Challenge:
Create a button on each of your "ending option" slides to bring the viewer back to the "choose an ending" page.

Presenting the Show:
1. Move to slide 1.
2. Pull down the Slide Show menu to View Show.
3. Click the mouse to move from one slide to the next.
4. Click the buttons to choose different story endings!

Extensions:
• Students can work in pairs or teams to complete the activity.
• Students can take a commonly known fairy tale or story and create alternate endings.

I'm Thankful For...

Grade Level:
- K (with help)
- 1 (with help)
- 2
- 3
- 4
- 5
- 6

Content Area:
Math
- Language Arts
- Social Studies
Science
- Cross Curricular

Multiple Intelligences:
- Verbal / Linguistic
Logical / Mathematical
Spatial
Bodily / Kinesthetic
Musical
- Interpersonal
- Intrapersonal
Naturalist

CD-ROM Templates:
• 36thankful.ppt - Microsoft PowerPoint

Overview:
In this activity, students will create 4 or 5 slides about things for which they are thankful. They will then share their creations in a slide show.

Software:
PowerPoint
(Or any slide show program such as Kid Pix, HyperStudio, or AppleWorks)

ISTE Standards:
• Students develop positive attitudes toward technology uses that support lifelong learning, collaboration, personal pursuits, and productivity.
• Students use technology tools to enhance learning, increase productivity, and promote creativity.

The Teacher's Role:
1. The teacher will lead a discussion with students about things they are thankful for.
2. The teacher will direct the students to write a list of 4 or 5 things they each are thankful for.
3. The teacher will demonstrate how to add text and graphics to a PowerPoint slide.
4. The teacher will demonstrate how to present the slides in a slide show.

Student Instructions:

Creating the Title Slide:
1. Open a new PowerPoint document.
2. Choose the Title Slide layout option.
3. Enter a title and your name.
4. Change the font size if you want.

Creating the slides
1. Pull down the **Insert** menu to **New Slide**.
2. Choose the Blank slide layout option.
3. Use the text tool to type one thing you are thankful for.
4. Use drawing tools, text tools, and/or clip art to create your design.
   a. If you don't see the drawing tools, pull down the **View** menu to **Toolbars** and pull over to **Drawing**.
   b. To add clip art, pull down the **Insert** menu to **Picture** and pull over to **Clip Art**.
5. Repeat steps 1-4 until you have created 4 or 5 slides.
6. SAVE!

Presenting the Show:
1. Pull down the **Slide Show** menu to **Slide Transition**.
2. Choose a transition from the pull down menu.
3. Click the "Apply to All" button.
4. Move to slide 1.
5. Pull down the **Slide Show** menu to **View Show**.
6. Click the mouse to move from one slide to the next.

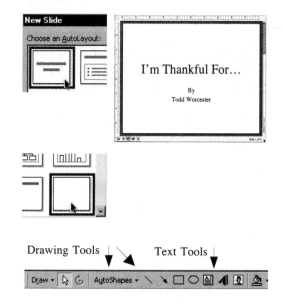

Drawing Tools   Text Tools

Extensions:
• Students could use a digital camera to take pictures of things they are thankful for. (Once the pictures are moved to the hard drive, pull down the Insert menu to Picture and pull over to From File.)
• Younger students could add pictures only (no text) to their slides.

Idiom Slide Show

37

Grade Level:
- K
- 1
- • 2
- • 3
- • 4
- • 5
- • 6

Content Area:
- Math
- • Language Arts
- • Social Studies
- Science
- • Cross Curricular

Multiple Intelligences:
- • Verbal / Linguistic
- • Logical / Mathematical
- Spatial
- Bodily / Kinesthetic
- Musical
- Interpersonal
- Intrapersonal
- • Naturalist

CD-ROM Templates:
• 37idiom.ppt - Microsoft PowerPoint

Overview:
In this activity, students will create slides to portray idioms or figures of speech and then will display them in a slide show.

Software:
Microsoft PowerPoint
(Other slide show programs such as Kid Pix, AppleWorks, or Hyperstudio)

ISTE Standards:
• Students develop positive attitudes toward technology uses that support lifelong learning, collaboration, personal pursuits, and productivity.
• Students use technology tools to enhance learning, increase productivity, and promote creativity.

Web Resources:
Funbrain's Paint by idioms - http://www.funbrain.com/idioms/
Idiom list - http://www.essdack.org/tips/idiomlst.html

The Teacher's Role:
1. The teacher will discuss idioms or figures of speech with the students.
2. The teacher will provide students with a list of idioms or will have the students brainstorm a list.
3. The teacher will instruct the students to create slides that contain images that portray idioms.

Student Instructions:
Creating the slides
1. Open a new blank PowerPoint slide.
2. Choose an idiom or figure of speech.
3. Use the drawing tools, text tools, and/or clip art to create an image that represents your idiom.
   a. If you don't see the drawing tools, pull down the **View** menu to **Toolbars** and pull over to **Drawing**.
   b. To add clip art, pull down the **Insert** menu to **Picture** and pull over to **Clip Art**.
4. To add a new slide, pull down the Insert menu to New Slide.
5. Repeat steps 2-4 until you have created 4 or 5 "idiom slides".
6. SAVE!

Drawing Tools   Text Tools

Presenting the Show:
1. Pull down the **Slide Show** menu to **Slide Transition**.
2. Choose a transition from the pull down menu.
3. Click the "Apply to All" button.
4. Move to slide 1.
5. Pull down the **Slide Show** menu to **View Show**.
6. Click the mouse to move from one slide to the next.

Extensions:
• Students could work in pairs or teams to complete the activity.
• Students can create their own series of slides for a slide show, or
• Each student can create ONE slide and the teacher can put the slides together into a slide show.
• Students could print their slides and bind together to create a book.

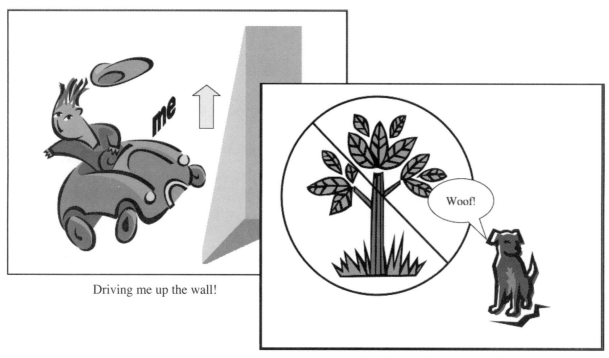

Driving me up the wall!

Barking up the wrong tree!

Sing-Along Slide Show

38

Grade Level:
- K
- 1
- 2
- 3
- 4
- 5
- 6

Content Area:
Math
- Language Arts
Social Studies
Science
- Cross Curricular (Music)

Multiple Intelligences:
- Verbal / Linguistic
Logical / Mathematical
- Spatial
Bodily / Kinesthetic
- Musical
Interpersonal
Intrapersonal
- Naturalist

CD-ROM Templates:
- 38music.ppt - Microsoft PowerPoint

Overview:
In this activity, students will create slides to portray the lyrics of a song. Then the slide show will be played in "synch" with the music as the students sing the song at a concert or performance.

Software:
PowerPoint
(Or any slide show program such as Kid Pix, HyperStudio, or AppleWorks)

ISTE Standards:
- Students develop positive attitudes toward technology uses that support lifelong learning, collaboration, personal pursuits, and productivity.
- Students use technology tools to enhance learning, increase productivity, and promote creativity.

The Teacher's Role:
1. The teacher will work with the music teacher in your school to choose a song that the students will sing at an upcoming performance.
   (Be sure to choose a song with a good, positive message.)
2. The teacher will print the words to the song and cut apart the "lines" of the lyrics.
   Important note -- Number the "lines" so you'll know the correct order.
3. The teacher will distribute the lines among the student.
4. The teacher will direct each student to create a slide with a picture that portrays their line of the song.
5. When students are finished, the teacher will put the slides into a slide show and add various transitions.
6. The teacher will use a projector or large screen display to show the slide show as the students sing the song.

Student Instructions:

Creating the slides

1. Open a new blank PowerPoint slide.
2. Use the drawing tools, text tools, and/or clip art to draw a picture that represents your line of the song.
   a. If you don't see the drawing tools, pull down the **View** menu to **Toolbars** and pull over to **Drawing**.
   b. To add clip art, pull down the **Insert** menu to **Picture** and pull over to **Clip Art**.
3. SAVE the slide with the number of your lyric AND your name.

Teacher Instructions:

Putting the slides together:

1. Have students save their slides to a network server or to a floppy disk (or other removable storage device).
2. Open the first student's document.
3. Move to the Slide Sorter view.
4. Select the slide.
5. Pull down the **Edit** menu to **Copy**.
6. Paste the slide into a "master" PowerPoint document.
7. Repeat until you have all slides in the master document.

Adding Transitions:

1. Move to slide 1.
2. Pull down the **Slide Show** menu to **Slide Transition**.
3. Choose a transition from the pull down menu.
4. Click the "Apply" button.
5. Move to the next slide.
6. Repeat steps 2-5 to choose transitions for each slide.

Presenting the Show:

1. Connect the computer to a projector so that it can be shown on a large screen above or beside the students as they sing.
2. Open the slide show.
3. Move to slide 1.
4. Pull down the **Slide Show** menu to **View Show**.
5. Click the mouse or use the right arrow on your keyboard to move from one slide to the next.

Extensions:

• Students could work in pairs or teams to complete the activity.
• Students could use digital pictures in their slide show.

Point of View Poem

39

Grade Level:
- K
- 1
- • 2
- • 3
- • 4
- • 5
- • 6

Content Area:
- Math
- • Language Arts
- • Social Studies
- Science
- • Cross Curricular

Multiple Intelligences:
- • Verbal / Linguistic
- • Logical / Mathematical
- Spatial
- Bodily / Kinesthetic
- Musical
- • Interpersonal
- Intrapersonal
- • Naturalist

CD-ROM Templates:
• 39pointofview - Kid Pix

Overview:
In this activity, students will choose a common, everyday object and then will look at that object from different points of view.

Software:
Kid Pix
Note: Instructions are provided for Kid Pix but can be adapted for PowerPoint, HyperStudio, AppleWorks, or other slide show programs.

ISTE Standards:
• Students develop positive attitudes toward technology uses that support lifelong learning, collaboration, personal pursuits, and productivity.
• Students use technology tools to enhance learning, increase productivity, and promote creativity.

The Teacher's Role:
Getting Ready
1. The teacher will lead a discussion about looking at things from different points of view.
2. The students could stand on their tables to see how the room looks different than when they are sitting in their chairs.
3. The teacher and students could discuss story characters' points of view: ex. How would you feel if you were Cinderella? What if you were one of the stepsisters?

Preparing for the slide show:
1. The teacher will explain the activity to the students and will share an example with them.
2. The teacher will demonstrate how to create the slides and the slide show.

Student Instructions:

Writing the Poem

1. Choose a common everyday object. (dog, cat, raindrop, chair, fire, pail of water, flower, bird, etc.)
2. Think about that object from different points of view.
3. Write a poem using this format:
   Line 1 = "What is a _____?".
   Line 2 = "A _____ is..."
   Lines 3 - 6 complete the sentence.

What is a raindrop?
A raindrop is...
... a breath of fresh air to a fish.
... an enemy to a window washer.
... an answer to a gardener's prayers.
... a shower for a duck.

Creating the slides

1. Open a new Kid Pix document.
2. Use the text tool to add text to the slide.
3. Add images to the slides:
   Use the tools at the left side of the screen and choose different options at the bottom of the screen draw pictures or "stamp" objects onto the screen.
4. Save the slide. (Pull down the **File** menu to **Save As** or click the disk icon.)
5. To get a new slide, pull down the **File** menu to **New**.

The slide show

1. Click the Slide Show icon at the bottom right corner of the screen to enter the slide show area.
2. Click the file folder icon below each slide to load the picture.
3. Click the movie projector icon to activate the other options.
4. Click the green arrow to choose a transition and/or sound.
5. After you've added all of the pictures and transitions, SAVE the slide show! (Pull down the **File** menu to **Save As** or click the disk icon.)
6. Click the green triangle (above the movie projector icon) to play the slide show.

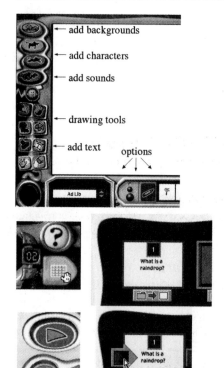

Extensions:

• Students could work in pairs or teams to complete the activity.
• Students could print their slides and bind them together to create a book.

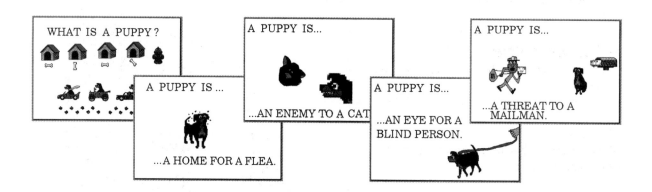

What Animal Am I?

40

Grade Level:
K
1
- 2
- 3
- 4
- 5
- 6

Content Area:
- Math
- Language Arts
- Social Studies
- Science
- Cross Curricular

Multiple Intelligences:
- Verbal / Linguistic
- Logical / Mathematical
  Spatial
  Bodily / Kinesthetic
  Musical
- Interpersonal
  Intrapersonal
- Naturalist

CD-ROM Templates:
40whatami.ppt - Microsoft PowerPoint

Overview:
In this activity, students will do research on an animal and will write 5 clues about it. They will put each clue on a separate slide and will reveal their animal at the end of the show.

Software:
Microsoft PowerPoint
Note: Instructions are provided for PowerPoint but can be adapted for Kid Pix, HyperStudio, AppleWorks, or other slide show programs.

ISTE Standards:
• Students use technology to locate, evaluate, and collect information from a variety of sources.
• Students use technology tools to enhance learning, increase productivity, and promote creativity.

Web Resources:
• Enchanted Learning Animal Printouts - http://www.EnchantedLearning.com/coloring/
• Sea World - http://www.seaworld.org/infobook.html
• Yahooligans Animals - http://www.yahooligans.com/content/animals/

The Teacher's Role:
1. The teacher will assist the students as they choose an animal.
2. The teacher will provide animal books and web resources.
3. The teacher will demonstrate how to copy a picture from the Internet.
4. The teacher will demonstrate how to create slides and add information to them.

Student Instructions:

Creating the Slide Show

1. Choose an animal and find some information about it using books or Internet resources.
2. Write 5 clues about your animal.
3. Open a blank PowerPoint slide show.
4. Create the following slides:
   Slide 1 - Add the text, "What Animal Am I?".
   Slide 2 - 6 - Enter a clue on each slide.
   Slide 7 - Add a picture of your animal and type "I am a _____."
       (See instructions below)

Capturing the Animal's Picture

1. Find a picture of the animal on the Internet.
2. Position your cursor directly over the image.
3. On a *Macintosh* computer, click and hold the mouse button (or control-click).
   On a *Windows* computer, click the right mouse button. A menu should appear.
4. Choose "Copy Image" or "Copy".
5. Move to your last PowerPoint slide.
6. Pull down the **Edit** menu to "**Paste**".

Sorting the Slides

You will want to present your slides so that your most general clue is first and your most specific clue is last. You can easily change the order of your slides:

1. Pull down the **View** menu to **Slide Sorter**.
2. Click and drag the slides into the order you want. (From general to specific.)
3. Pull down the **View** menu to **Normal**.
4. SAVE!

Presenting the Show:

1. Pull down the **Slide Show** menu to **Slide Transition**.
2. Choose a transition from the pull down menu.
3. Click the "Apply to All" button.
4. Move to slide 1.
5. Pull down the **Slide Show** menu to **View Show**.
6. Click the mouse to move from one slide to the next.

Extensions:

• Students can create similar slide shows for any person, place, thing, animal, etc.: What am I? Who am I? Where am I?
• For a math activity, students could create a "What number am I" slide show with clues like: I'm greater than 10; I can be divided by 2; I'm less than 30; both of my digits are the same.
• Slide shows can be printed to create books or mini-books. (See instructions for State Minibooks on page 21.

Classmates Crossword

Grade Level:
K
1
- 2
- 3
- 4
- 5
- 6

Content Area:
Math
- Language Arts
- Social Studies
Science
- Cross Curricular

Multiple Intelligences:
- Verbal / Linguistic
- Logical / Mathematical
Spatial
Bodily / Kinesthetic
Musical
- Interpersonal
Intrapersonal
Naturalist

CD-ROM Templates:
- 41crossword.pdf - Adobe Acrobat

Overview:
In this activity, students will use an online tool to create a crossword puzzle using names and "clues" about their classmates.

Software:
Internet Browser such as Internet Explorer or Netscape Navigator

ISTE Standards:
- Use keyboards and other common input and output devices efficiently and effectively.
- Use technology tools for individual and collaborative writing, communication, and publishing activities.

Web Resources:
Puzzlemaker - http://www.puzzlemaker.com

The Teacher's Role:
1. The teacher will divide the class list in to groups of 8-12 students.
2. The teacher will give each student a list of 8-12 other students in the class.
3. The teacher will instruct the students to think of a clue for each student on their list.
   (Remind them that the clues should be positive!)
4. The teacher will show the students how to create a criss cross puzzle using the Puzzlemaker web site.
5. The teacher will demonstrate how to print the puzzles.
6. After everyone is finished, the teacher will distribute the puzzles at random and let students solve the puzzles.

Student Instructions:

1. Write a clue for each classmate on your list. (Make sure the clues are positive!)
2. Open the Puzzlemaker Web site. www.puzzlemaker.com
3. Select the Criss-Cross Puzzle from the pull-down menu.
4. Follow the on-screen prompts to enter a title, the number of squares, and the size of the square.
5. Enter the name of each classmate followed by your clue.
6. Click the Create button. (Create a Printable Version)
7. Print.

Extensions:

- Students could create crosswords using vocabulary words and definitions for any content area.
- Students could create puzzles about themselves and/or their family.
- Students might want to try other types of puzzles at the Puzzlemaker site.

▸ Select a puzzle from the pull-down menu:

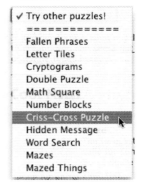

✓ Try other puzzles!
= = = = = = = = = = = = =
Fallen Phrases
Letter Tiles
Cryptograms
Double Puzzle
Math Square
Number Blocks
Criss-Cross Puzzle
Hidden Message
Word Search
Mazes
Mazed Things

STEP 1.
Enter the title of your criss-cross puzzle
The title will appear at the top of your page. IMPORTANT: Puzzle titles are limited to 49 characters.

Classmates Crossword

STEP 2.
Enter the number of squares for your puzzle
Width 50   Height 50

STEP 3.
Enter the size of the square
Specify the size of each square. 30 is standard size.
Square size 30

STEP 4.
Enter the words and clues
On each line enter a word followed by a space and then the clue for that word.

Lisa has a cast on her left arm
Jerry tells funny jokes
Jordan has the longest hair in the class
Todd moved here this year

[Reset] [Create a Printable Version]

Classmates Crossword

Across
4. has a dog named Sox
5. likes to skateboard
8. lives on a dairy farm
9. moved here this year
10. the tallest girl in the class
Down
1. wears glasses
2. has braces
3. has a cast on her left arm
6. wears his hat backwards
7. tells funny jokes
8. has the longest hair in the class
9. has five brothers

Weather Cryptogram

42

Grade Level:
K
1
• 2
• 3
• 4
• 5
• 6

Content Area:
Math
• Language Arts
Social Studies
• Science
• Cross Curricular

Multiple Intelligences:
• Verbal / Linguistic
• Logical / Mathematical
Spatial
Bodily / Kinesthetic
Musical
Interpersonal
Intrapersonal
• Naturalist

CD-ROM Templates:
• 42cryptogram.pdf - Adobe Acrobat Reader

Overview:
In this activity, students will use an online cryptogram creator to design and print a weather cryptogram.

Software:
Internet Browser such as Internet Explorer or Netscape Navigator

ISTE Standards:
• Students use a variety of media and formats to communicate information and ideas effectively to multiple audiences.
• Students develop positive attitudes toward technology uses that support lifelong learning, collaboration, personal pursuits, and productivity.

Web Resources:
Awesome Clip Art for Kids - http://www.awesomeclipartforkids.com/

The Teacher's Role:
1. The teacher will provide students with the link to the cryptogram creator site. (www.awesomeclipartforkids.com/)
2. The teacher will show the students how to create a cryptogram.
3. The teacher will print an example cryptogram to show students.
4. The teacher will help the class to brainstorm a list of weather words.
5. The teacher will write the words on the chalkboard or white board or write on paper and copy for students. (OR - use the Inspiration program to record the brainstormed words.)

Student Instructions:

Getting Ready:
1. Brainstorm and record a list of weather words with your classmates or teammates.
2. Choose one word from the list and write a question or clue for it.
3. Open the Web Site: www.awesomeclipartforkids.com/.
4. Click the Cryptogram Makers link in the Worksheets & Puzzles area.
5. Choose to create a Weather Cryptogram.

Creating the Cryptogram:
(See example below)
1. Enter a title for your cryptogram.
2. Enter up to nine words from word list. (NOTE - do not include the word you chose in Step 2 above.)
3. Enter your riddle. This is the question or clue you wrote in step 2 above.
4. Enter the word that answers the riddle.
5. Choose a title graphic and separator line.
6. Click the Make Puzzle button.
7. Click the Show Worksheet button.
8. Print.
9. If you want, you can also Show Answer Key and print it.

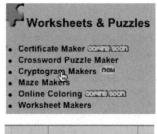

Extensions:
• Students could create cryptograms using vocabulary words from all content areas.
• Students could create an "all about me" cryptogram, including words and a riddle that describes them.

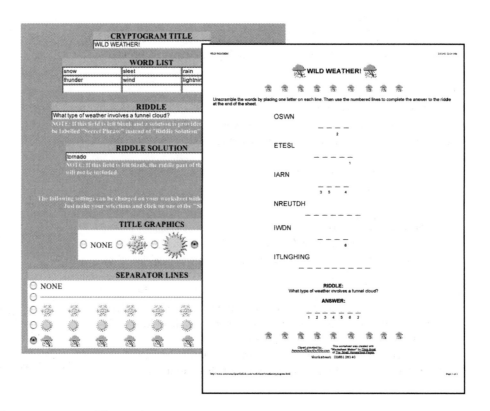

Teacher's Helper Hotlists

43

Grade Level:
K
1
2
• 3
• 4
• 5
• 6

Content Area:
• Math
• Language Arts
• Social Studies
• Science
• Cross Curricular

Multiple Intelligences:
• Verbal / Linguistic
• Logical / Mathematical
  Spatial
  Bodily / Kinesthetic
  Musical
• Interpersonal
  Intrapersonal
  Naturalist

CD-ROM Templates:
• 43hotlist.doc - Microsoft Word
• 43hotlist.cwk - AppleWorks

Overview:
The teachers in your school probably don't have enough time to find Web resources for topics they teach. You and your students can help! Students can search the Internet for appropriate web sites and then can create lists of addresses (hotlists).

Software:
Microsoft Word or AppleWorks Word Processing
Internet Browser such as Netscape Navigator or Internet Explorer

ISTE Standards:
• Students use technology to locate, evaluate, and collect information from a variety of sources.
• Students practice responsible use of technology systems, information, and software.

Web Resources:
Educational Resources:
Kathy Schrock's Guide - http://school.discovery.com/schrockguide/
Eduhound - http://www.eduhound.com/mainpage.cfm
Search Tools:
Yahooligans - www.yahooligans.com
KidsClick - www.kidsclick.org

The Teacher's Role:
1. The teacher will send an email to other teachers in your building, asking what topics they will cover throughout the rest of the school year. Compile a list of topics.
2. The teacher will help the students to choose a topic from the list.
3. The teacher will demonstrate how to find information on the Internet.
4. The teacher will show the students how to copy a web address and paste it into their word processing document.
5. The teacher will demonstrate how to turn the address into a hyperlink.
6. The teacher will email the completed hotlists back to the teachers.

Student Instructions:

Setting up the hotlist document:
1. Choose a topic from the list your teacher has provided.
2. Open a word processing document.
3. Add a title at the top of the page.

Creating the hotlist:

1. Browse or search the Internet to find a topic-related Web site that would be helpful to the teacher and students. Make sure the Web sites are easy to navigate, quick to load, appropriate for kids, and attractive
2. Highlight the web address. See image at right.
3. Pull down the **Edit** menu to **Copy**.
4. Return to your word processing document.
5. Enter the title of the Web site you found. Press the Return/Enter or Tab Key
6. Pull down the **Edit** menu to **Paste**. This will paste the Web address you copied earlier.
7. Repeat steps 1-5 until you have added at least 5 addresses to your document.
8. SAVE!

Hyperlinking the addresses:
Microsoft Word:
Place your cursor at the end of an address and press the Return or Enter key on your keyboard. This will turn your address into a hyperlink!

AppleWorks:
1. Pull down the **Window** menu to **Show Button Bar**.
2. Highlight the first web address on your page.
3. Pull down the **Edit** menu to **Copy**.
3. Click the Insert Hyperlink button.
4. Insert your cursor in the URL area.
5. Pull down the **Edit** menu to **Paste**.
6. Repeat for remaining web addresses.

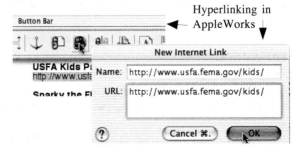

Hyperlinking in AppleWorks

Extensions:
• Students could add clip art and change the fonts / sizes to make their "hotlist" more attractive.
• Students could provide questions along with the links to create scavenger hunt activities.

Online Mad Libs

44

Grade Level:
K
1
- 2
- 3
- 4
- 5
- 6

Content Area:
Math
- Language Arts
Social Studies
Science
- Cross Curricular

Multiple Intelligences:
- Verbal / Linguistic
Logical / Mathematical
Spatial
Bodily / Kinesthetic
Musical
Interpersonal
Intrapersonal
Naturalist

Overview:
In this activity, students will follow the online prompts to enter random nouns, adjectives, adverbs, etc. Then their words are inserted to create a silly story.

Software:
Internet Browser such as Internet Explorer or Netscape Navigator

ISTE Standards:
- Use keyboards and other common input and output devices efficiently and effectively.
- Use technology tools for individual and collaborative writing, communication, and publishing activities.

Web Resources:
Wacky Web Tales - http://www.eduplace.com/tales/
Wacky Tales - http://www.funbrain.com/wacky/
Word Central Verse Composer - www.wordcentral.com (enter the music room)

To find others, do a web search for "mad libs" or "mad libs for kids".

The Teacher's Role:
1. The teacher will provide students with links to mad lib web sites.
2. The teacher will demonstrate how to create a mad lib.
3. The teacher will demonstrate how to print the mad lib (optional).

Student Instructions:

1. Open your web browser and go to one of the following sites:
   • Wacky Web Tales - http://www.eduplace.com/tales/
   • Wacky Tales - http://www.funbrain.com/wacky/
   • Word Central Verse Composer - www.wordcentral.com (enter the music room)
2. Follow the online instructions to choose a story.
3. Use the prompts to enter words. Be creative!
4. Create the story.
5. Print!

Extensions:

• Students could create their own mad libs and exchange with each other.
• Students can work in groups to create mad libs.
• If a projector or large screen display is available, the entire class can create a mad lib together.

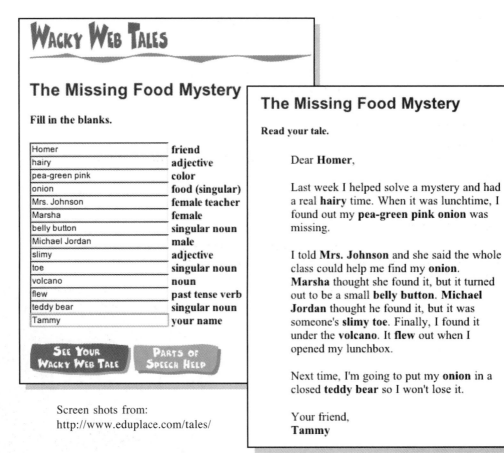

WACKY WEB TALES

The Missing Food Mystery

Fill in the blanks.

Homer	friend
hairy	adjective
pea-green pink	color
onion	food (singular)
Mrs. Johnson	female teacher
Marsha	female
belly button	singular noun
Michael Jordan	male
slimy	adjective
toe	singular noun
volcano	noun
flew	past tense verb
teddy bear	singular noun
Tammy	your name

SEE YOUR WACKY WEB TALE   PARTS OF SPEECH HELP

The Missing Food Mystery

Read your tale.

Dear **Homer**,

Last week I helped solve a mystery and had a real **hairy** time. When it was lunchtime, I found out my **pea-green pink onion** was missing.

I told **Mrs. Johnson** and she said the whole class could help me find my **onion**. **Marsha** thought she found it, but it turned out to be a small **belly button**. **Michael Jordan** thought he found it, but it was someone's **slimy toe**. Finally, I found it under the **volcano**. It **flew** out when I opened my lunchbox.

Next time, I'm going to put my **onion** in a closed **teddy bear** so I won't lose it.

Your friend,
Tammy

Screen shots from:
http://www.eduplace.com/tales/

45

Interactive Internet Activities

Grade Level:
- K
- 1
- 2
- 3
- 4
- 5
- 6

Content Area:
- Math
- Language Arts
- Social Studies
- Science
- Cross Curricular

Multiple Intelligences:
- Verbal / Linguistic
- Logical / Mathematical
- Spatial
- Bodily / Kinesthetic
- Musical
  Interpersonal
  Intrapersonal
- Naturalist

Overview:
Sometimes students need to use the computer for fun! This activity provides the students with a variety of Interactive web resources that are entertaining AND educational! These activities are great for early finishers or for reward days in the computer lab.

Software:
Internet Browser such as Internet Explorer or Netscape Navigator

ISTE Standards:
- Students develop positive attitudes toward technology uses that support lifelong learning, collaboration, personal pursuits, and productivity.

Web Resources:
- See the following Page
- Find additional web resources by searching for interactive educational games or online educational activities.

The Teacher's Role:
1. The teacher will provide students with links to educational online activities.
   (You may want to set bookmarks or hyperlinks for young students.)
2. The teacher will supervise the students while they are online!
3. The teacher will provide alternatives for students who do not have permission to use the internet.

Student Instructions:

Have fun at some of these Web sites:

FunSchool
www.funschool.com

FunBrain
www.funbrain.com

Crayola
www.crayola.com

Prongo
www.prongo.com

Scholastic
http://www.scholastic.com/kids/

Personalized Stories

Grade Level:
- K
- 1
- 2
- 3
- 4
- 5
- 6

Content Area:
- Math
- Language Arts
- Social Studies
- Science
- Cross Curricular

Multiple Intelligences:
- Verbal / Linguistic
- Logical / Mathematical
- Spatial
- Bodily / Kinesthetic
- Musical
- Interpersonal
- Intrapersonal
- Naturalist

Overview:
In this online activity, students can create and print personalized stories!

Software:
Internet

ISTE Standards:
- Use keyboards and other common input and output devices efficiently and effectively.
- Use technology tools for individual and collaborative writing, communication, and publishing activities.

Web Resources:
Note - web addresses are subject to change. To find alternate storybooks, use a search tool to search for "interactive personalized story".

Huggies - http://www.huggies.com/happybabyfun/storybook/
Sears Portrait Studio - www.searsportrait.com (click the children's stories link)
Bing Puddlepot - www.bingpuddlepot.com/story.asp

The Teacher's Role:
1. The teacher will help the students find the appropriate web site. (You may want to set a Favorite or Bookmark for the site.)
2. The teacher will assist the students as they follow the on-screen prompts to create their stories.

Student Instructions:

1. The following are web sites that allow you to create personalized stories. Open one of them:

   Huggies - http://www.huggies.com/happybabyfun/storybook/
   Sears Portrait Studio - www.searsportrait.com (click the children's stories link)
   Bing Puddlepot - www.bingpuddlepot.com/story.asp

2. Follow the on-screen prompts to create a personalized story.
3. Print the story.
   If the story has multiple pages, print and then staple together to create a book.
   or
   Punch a hole in a corner (or punch two holes on the side) and tie a ribbon through the pages to hold them together.

Extensions:

• Students could create personalized stories for their friends.
• The teacher could put the students' names in a hat. Each student could draw a name and then creates a personalized story for that classmate.
• Older students could create their own story in a word processing document and then use the Find and Replace command to personalize it for different students.

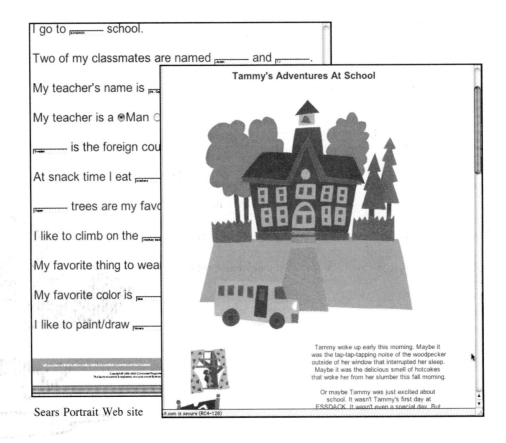

Sears Portrait Web site

Coupon Booklets

47

Grade Level:
- K (with help)
- 1 (with help)
- 2
- 3
- 4
- 5
- 6

Content Area:
Math
- Language Arts
- Social Studies
Science
- Cross Curricular

Multiple Intelligences:
- Verbal / Linguistic
Logical / Mathematical
- Spatial
Bodily / Kinesthetic
Musical
- Interpersonal
- Intrapersonal
Naturalist

CD-ROM Templates:
• 47coupon.ppt - Microsoft PowerPoint

Overview:
In this activity, students create and print coupon booklets to give as a gift to Mom, Dad, Teacher, Grandparent, etc.

Software:
Microsoft PowerPoint

ISTE Standards:
• Use keyboards and other common input and output devices efficiently and effectively.
• Use technology tools for individual and collaborative writing, communication, and publishing activities.

The Teacher's Role:
1. The teacher will lead a discussion about helping others.
2. The teacher will assist the students as they list 5 things to put on their coupons.
3. The teacher will show how to create coupon slides in PowerPoint.
4. The teacher will demonstrate how to print the slides 6-per-page.
5. The teacher will show students how to cut and staple their booklets.

Student Instructions:

Slide 1:
1. Open a new PowerPoint document.
2. Choose the Blank slide layout option.
3. Use the drawing tools, text tools, and/or clip art to create the title page of your booklet.
   a. If you don't see the drawing tools, pull down the **View** menu to **Toolbars** and pull over to **Drawing**.
   b. To add clip art, pull down the **Insert** menu to **Picture** and pull over to **Clip Art**.

Slides 2-6:
1. Pull down the **Insert** menu to **New Slide**.
2. Add text and images to your slide to create a coupon.
3. Repeat steps 1 and 2 for each slide.
4. SAVE!

Finishing the Mini-Book
1. Pull down the **File** menu to **Print**.
2. In the PowerPoint print options, choose to print handouts at 6 per page.
3. Print.
4. Cut around slides, adding 1/2 inch to the left side of each.
   Note - Look at the dotted lines in the image at the right to see where to cut.
5. Staple the coupons together to create a booklet!

Extensions:
• The teacher could create a booklet for students including things like: • free assignment; • 10 points extra credit; • late assignment; etc.
• The teacher could use tag board to create a stencil for cutting. Students could place the stencil over their page and then draw lines to show where to cut.

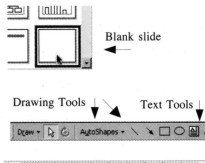

Blank slide

Drawing Tools   Text Tools

The dotted lines show where you should cut:

Staple slides together to create a coupon booklet. ➔

Key Ring for Dad

48

Grade Level:
- K
- 1
- 2
- 3
- 4
- 5
- 6

Content Area:
Math
Language Arts
Social Studies
Science
- Cross Curricular

Multiple Intelligences:
- Verbal / Linguistic
  Logical / Mathematical
- Spatial
- Bodily / Kinesthetic
  Musical
- Interpersonal
  Intrapersonal
  Naturalist

CD-ROM Templates:
• 48keyring.ppt - Microsoft PowerPoint

Overview:
Students will design and print shrink art key rings to give to their fathers (or another male adult.)

Software:
Microsoft PowerPoint

ISTE Standards:
• Students develop positive attitudes toward technology uses that support lifelong learning, collaboration, personal pursuits, and productivity.
• Students use technology tools to enhance learning, increase productivity, and promote creativity.

The Teacher's Role:
1. The teacher will instruct the students to write a nice sentence or a short poem about their fathers (or other male adult).
2. The teacher will provide printable shrink sheets. (Available in the labels section of a business supply store or discount store.)
3. The teacher will show the students how to create their key ring design using PowerPoint.
4. The teacher will divide the students into groups of 4.
5. The teacher will proof the students' creations before printing.
6. The teacher will print the shrink sheets (four per page).
7. The teacher will bake the designs to shrink them.

NOTE - To conserve shrink art sheets, use the PowerPoint option to print as Handouts - 4 per sheet. Therefore, four students should take turns on one computer to create their key rings.

Student Instructions:
Student 1:
1. Open a blank PowerPoint slide.
2. Click the AutoShapes button; pull up to Basic Shapes; and pull over to choose a shape.
3. Click and drag to create the shape. (The shape should fill most of the slide.)
4. Click the arrow beside the paint bucket to change the color of the shape.
5. Use the Word art or Text Box to add text.
6. Move and resize the text until it fits over the shape.
7. SAVE!

Students 2, 3, and 4:
1. Pull down the **Insert** menu to **New Slide**; choose a blank slide.
2. Click the AutoShapes button; pull up to Basic Shapes; and pull over to choose a shape.
3. Click and drag to create the shape. (The shape should fill most of the slide.)
4. Click the arrow beside the paint bucket to change the color of the shape.
5. Use the Word art or Text Box to add text.
6. Move and resize the text until it fits over the shape.
7. SAVE!

Printing the Key Rings:
1. Have your teacher check your spelling.
2. With the teacher's help, put a shrink art sheet in the printer.
3. Pull down the **File** menu to **Print**.
4. Choose the Handout option - 4 per page.
5. Print onto shrink art sheet.
6. Use scissors to cut around the shapes.
7. Use a paper punch to punch a hole in the key ring.
8. Follow the instructions on the shrink sheets package to bake the designs.

Extensions:
• Students could create key rings with any design for any occasion.
• Students could print digital pictures onto key rings.

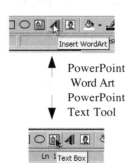

PowerPoint
Word Art
PowerPoint
Text Tool

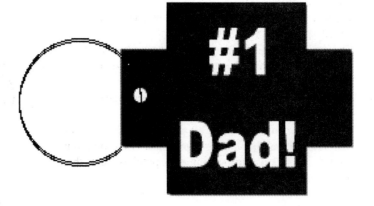

Magnet for Mother

Grade Level:
- K
- 1
- 2
- 3
- 4
- 5
- 6

Content Area:
Math
Language Arts
Social Studies
Science
- Cross Curricular

Multiple Intelligences:
- Verbal / Linguistic
  Logical / Mathematical
- Spatial
- Bodily / Kinesthetic
  Musical
- Interpersonal
  Intrapersonal
  Naturalist

CD-ROM Templates:
- 49magnet.ppt - Microsoft PowerPoint

Overview:
Students will design and print magnets to give as gifts to their mothers.

Software:
Microsoft PowerPoint

ISTE Standards:
- Students develop positive attitudes toward technology uses that support lifelong learning, collaboration, personal pursuits, and productivity.
- Students use technology tools to enhance learning, increase productivity, and promote creativity.

The Teacher's Role:
1. The teacher will instruct the students to write a nice sentence or a short poem about their mothers (or other female adult).
2. The teacher will provide printable magnet sheets. (Available in the labels section of a business supply store or discount store.)
3. The teacher will show the students how to create their magnet using PowerPoint.
4. The teacher will divide the students into groups of 4.
5. The teacher will proof the students' creations before printing.
6. The teacher will print the magnets (four per page).

NOTE - To conserve magnet sheets, use the PowerPoint option to print as Handouts - 4 per sheet. Therefore, four students should take turns on one computer to create their magnets.

Student Instructions:

Student 1:
1. Open a blank PowerPoint slide.
2. Click the AutoShapes button; pull up to Basic Shapes; and pull over to choose a shape.
3. Click and drag to create the shape. (The shape should fill most of the slide.)
4. Click the arrow beside the paint bucket to change the color of the shape.
5. Use the Word art or Text Box to add text.
6. Move and resize the text until it fits over the shape.
7. SAVE!

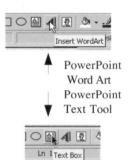

PowerPoint
Word Art
PowerPoint
Text Tool

Students 2, 3, and 4:
1. Pull down the **Insert** menu to **New Slide**; choose a blank slide.
2. Click the **AutoShapes** button; pull up to **Basic Shapes**; and pull over to choose a shape.
3. Click and drag to create the shape. (The shape should fill most of the slide.)
4. Click the arrow beside the paint bucket to change the color of the shape.
5. Use the Word Art or Text Box to add text.
6. Move and resize the text until it fits over the shape.
7. SAVE!

Printing the Magnets:
1. Have your teacher check your spelling.
2. With the teacher's help, put a magnet sheet in the printer.
3. Pull down the **File** menu to **Print**.
4. Choose the Handout option - 4 per page.
5. Print onto magnet sheet.
6. Use scissors to cut around the shapes.

Extensions:
• Students could create magnets with any design for any occasion.
• Students could print digital pictures onto magnets.

Sun Catchers

50

Grade Level:
- K
- 1
- 2
- 3
- 4
- 5
- 6

Content Area:
Math
Language Arts
Social Studies
Science
- Cross Curricular

Multiple Intelligences:
- Verbal / Linguistic
  Logical / Mathematical
- Spatial
- Bodily / Kinesthetic
  Musical
- Interpersonal
  Intrapersonal
  Naturalist

CD-ROM Templates:
- 50suncatchers.ppt - Microsoft PowerPoint

Overview:
Students will design a sun catcher and will print it onto window decal sheets.

Software:
Microsoft PowerPoint

ISTE Standards:
- Students develop positive attitudes toward technology uses that support
  lifelong learning, collaboration, personal pursuits, and productivity.
- Students use technology tools to enhance learning, increase productivity,
  and promote creativity.

The Teacher's Role:
1. The teacher will instruct the students to write or choose a
   nice phrase to put on their sun catcher.
2. The teacher will provide printable window decal sheets.
   (Available in the labels section of a business supply store
   or discount store.)
3. The teacher will show the students how to create their sun
   catcher using PowerPoint.
4. The teacher will divide the students into groups of 4.
5. The teacher will proof the students' creations before
   printing.
6. The teacher will print the sun catchers (four per page).

NOTE - To conserve decal sheets, use the PowerPoint
option to print as Handouts - 4 per sheet. Therefore, four
students should take turns on one computer to create their
sun catchers.

Student Instructions:

Student 1:

1. Open a blank PowerPoint slide.
2. Click the AutoShapes button; pull up to Basic Shapes; and pull over to choose a shape.
3. Click and drag to create the shape. (The shape should fill most of the slide.)
4. Click the arrow beside the paint bucket to change the color of the shape.
5. Use the Word art or Text Box to add text.
6. Move and resize the text until it fits over the shape.
7. SAVE!

Students 2, 3, and 4:

1. Pull down the **Insert** menu to **New Slide**; choose a blank slide.
2. Click the AutoShapes button; pull up to Basic Shapes; and pull over to choose a shape.
3. Click and drag to create the shape. (The shape should fill most of the slide.)
4. Click the arrow beside the paint bucket to change the color of the shape.
5. Use the Word art or Text Box to add text.
6. Move and resize the text until it fits over the shape.
7. SAVE!

Printing the Sun catcher:

1. Have your teacher check your spelling.
2. With the teacher's help, put a decal sheet in the printer.
3. Pull down the File menu to Print.
4. Choose the Handout option - 4 per page.
5. Print onto decal sheet.
6. Use scissors to cut around the shapes.

PowerPoint
Word Art
PowerPoint
Text Tool

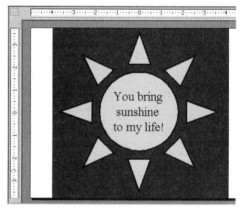

Extensions:

• Students could create decals with any design for any occasion.
• Students could create school spirit decals.
• Students could create decals to support reading.

DATE DUE
